90 Days to a High-Performance Team

90 Days to a High-Performance Team

A Complete Problem-Solving Strategy to Help Your Team Thrive in Any Environment

- Function in Lean or Chaotic Times
- Eliminate Rivalries and Miscommunications
- Manage Your Poor Performers

Chris DeVany

New York   Chicago   San Francisco   Lisbon   London   Madrid   Mexico City   Milan   New Delhi   San Juan   Seoul   Singapore   Sydney   Toronto

Library of Congress Cataloging-in-Publication Data

DeVany, Chris (Christopher R.)
    90 days to a high-performance team: a complete problem-solving
strategy to help your team thrive in any environment/by Chris DeVany.
      p.   cm.
   ISBN 978-0-07-162940-9 (alk. paper)
    1. Teams in the workplace—Management. 2. Supervision of employees.
I. Title. II. Title: Ninety days to a high-performance team.

   HD66.D472 2009
   658.4'022—dc22   2009027023

This book was set in Minion and Formata by Robert S. Tinnon Design

Interior design by Robert S. Tinnon
Interior illustrations by Randy Miyake

Dedication

I WOULD LIKE TO DEDICATE THIS BOOK TO MY WIFE, Jean Ann, and to her father, Al Schulte. Jean Ann has been a remarkably supportive partner in all my endeavors, most especially starting and growing my management consulting firm, Pinnacle Performance Improvement Worldwide. Jean Ann also provides me daily with the emotional support I think all of us need to make a healthy relationship continue to grow.

In also dedicating this book to Al Schulte, it gives me the opportunity to recognize a very special man. Before, while, and after becoming my father-in-law, this devoted husband and father took on a number of challenges and persevered, including some of the challenges we entrepreneurs face. He opened several pharmacies in economically disadvantaged and African American neighborhoods where it was highly unpopular to start a business (while we were still in the midst of the Great Depression!), had the courage to open one of the first pharmacies in the country located inside a department store, and was the sole breadwinner for a family of five, while still having the very big and warm heart to constantly and perhaps daily help those in need. Al also gave both my wife and me a big "leg up" on getting our financial lives off the ground, for which I will be forever grateful.

Contents

CHAPTER SIX

"The Boss from Hell": Help Is on the Way!   67

CHAPTER SEVEN

**Your Team Is Clashing with Another Team—Getting Everyone on
the Same Page   77**

CHAPTER TEN

**From Forming to Performing: The Top Ten Ways to Develop a
Managing "Rhythm" That Works for You and Your Team   127**

Acknowledgments

KNOWING THAT I WILL FORGET SOME, let me start by thanking Richard Binkowski, Harry Dawson, and Father Anthony Kulig. Mr. Binkowski inspired me as a high school sophomore and senior to read with gusto and write with eloquence. Mr. Dawson guided and inspired many Seton Hall Prep students to read a playwright's words with focus, to appreciate the characters as written, and to adopt the character we were portraying as ourselves. Both gentlemen also helped me learn that teaching, for which I am often engaged by clients, is also about entertaining, as is writing. Father Kulig taught me that having and applying a passion is important in everything you do, in this case acting and performing ("He's a music man, he's a music man . . .").

A few other acknowledgments at this time: my darling wife, Jean Ann, for her unwavering support; my mom and dad for raising me so well by example; and countless others for your faith and trust in hiring me to consult your managers, to provide professional development instruction, to speak at your conferences, to facilitate strategic planning and group process, and to earn a living, which is fulfilling every day.

Introduction:
How to Use This Book

THIS BOOK IS DESIGNED TO HELP ANYONE and everyone who has been tasked with managing a team. It is intended to read just as if you, the reader, and I were in the same office. Please use this resource as it is designed: as a hands-on manager's helper. And in the spirit of hands-on help, if you have any questions as you read this, just shoot me an e-mail at cdevany@ppiw.com.

Remember, this book is designed to help you address ten key team performance aspects, plus additional tools and resources, including:

- Managing a team
- Customer service
- Communication
- Facilitating change
- Removing troublemakers
- Managing your boss
- Clashes between two teams
- Managing performance
- Budgeting
- Taking a team from any of three stages to peak performance
- Managing virtual teams
- Coaching for peak performance

When examining your own team for possible areas of improvement, it helps to consider what makes for a successful team in the first place! Here are some general definitions that will help order your thinking.

I suggest the following approach for reading and using this work:

1. Immediately read and implement suggestions in Chapter One (Managing a Team) from "Before You Start," "The First Day," and "The First Week."
2. As soon as you can, no later than the first weekend, visit the "Before You Start" sections of each chapter to give yourself a sense of where to start, as well as a roadmap for prioritizing which of these 10 "issues" are your highest priorities.
3. I further suggest you identify no more than three "Top Priorities" from these issues and start tackling them.
4. In each chapter, you will find a Manager's Action Plan and Manager's Time-Out. Use the Action Plan for . . . well, you know . . . and use the Time-Out for reading, reflection, and enhancing your understanding.

Characteristics of Effective Teams

Within the corporate setting, team collaborations are not a new concept. However, in a rapidly changing marketplace, more emphasis is being placed on their success. We will use the term *community* in a corporate context, because team building means building a sense of community.

To help us better understand this team-building process and our terms, please review the following definitions of the characteristics of effective teams.

Goals

Collaborations need goals in order to be effective. Clear, elevating goals provide the member with a sense of worthiness, opportunity, challenge, consequence, identification, and appeal. These goals are related to the needs and are achievable, thus appealing to that sense of purpose in which humans operate. Goals allow members to buy into what the collaboration is doing. There is an interdependency among members because they rely on one another for the achievement of the group's goals. Goals are most effective when written down and agreed upon.

Communication

Collaborative efforts are dependent upon open and clear communication. A formal process for communication between meetings must be established, as well as communication from the collaboration to the broader community. Establishing and maintaining nonformal communication channels with local community leaders will also be essential. Marketing of the collaboration efforts must be conducted in order to obtain community support and acquire needed resources.

Sustainability

In order for collaborative efforts to be sustainable, it is essential that systems be instituted to provide sustained membership, resources, and strategic program planning. Resource development efforts must be ongoing to assure that the appropriate levels of revenue, time, and people are available to conduct the group's programming efforts. Planning must be both short term and long term. The collaboration must be able to identify emerging trends and issues and develop strategies for needed expansion.

Research and Evaluation

Obtaining and utilizing information is essential for collaborative groups. Data must be collected which established benchmarks for future impact and outcome analysis. Evaluation efforts are essential to monitor progress related to the group's goals and objectives and to make modifications where necessary. Strategies for communicating program impacts must be established.

Political Climate

Political climate is the history and environment surrounding power and decision making. Political climate may be within the community as a whole, systems within the community, or networks of people. A healthy collaboration ensures that political climates affecting or potentially affecting the collaboration have been identified and utilized in the positive development of the collaboration. A wide cross-section of people, groups, and organizations within the identified political climate will better ensure a mutually inclusive membership within the collaboration. It is important that a collaboration has members who know which decision makers need to be influenced and how to influence those decision makers.

Resources

Resources refers to four types of capital: environmental, in-kind, financial, and human. An environment where there is connectedness at all levels—as a history of working together; as a supportive political climate; and policies, laws, and regulations that encourage cooperativeness—increases the probability of a successful collaboration. The contribution of human capital to a collaboration is a crucial investment for sustainability.

Catalysts

Catalysts get the collaboration started. The existing problem(s) or the reason(s) for the collaboration to exist must be viewed by the community and potential collaboration members as a situation that requires a comprehensive response. In addition to a community-wide issue, the second type of catalyst needed is a convener. This is a person who calls the initial meeting of a collaboration and draws everyone into a dialogue about possible solutions to the situation. Conveners must have organizational and interpersonal skills, and must carry out the role with passion and fairness.

Policies, Laws, and Regulations

Solving problems collaboratively means transforming and changing policies, laws, and regulations. Collaborations are more likely to succeed when supportive policies, laws, and regulations are in place. Sustainability of collaborations is often dependent on policies and practices in place.

History

History has to do with a community's past with regard to working cooperatively or competitively. Collaboration is more likely to succeed in communities that have a history of working together cooperatively (Mattessich & Monsey, 1992). In communities where a history of cooperation exists, the collaboration members trust each other and the collaboration process. Collaborations succeed in an environment that is oriented toward cooperation and away from competition.

Connectedness

Connectedness refers to the linkages among individuals, groups, and organizations. It is how people know each other or how they are connected to one another. There are multiple types of connections that are not mutually exclusive. Collaborations that employ both the formal and informal networks of communication to support them are more likely to succeed.

Collaborations that are effective involve well-connected individuals, groups, organizations, and communities and have established informal and formal communication networks at all levels of connectedness.

Leadership

Community collaboration requires effective leadership. While leadership is often defined as who is in power, the definition of leadership for successful collaborations is broadened to include those who impact change within their community, group, and/or organization. Norms of operations must be established that include protocol, conflict resolution, political and cultural sensitivity, structure, and roles and responsibilities. Leadership should facilitate and support team building and capitalize upon diversity and individual, group, and organizational strengths.

Community Development

Community development is the process of mobilizing communities to address important issues and build upon the strengths of the community. The collaboration begins the process of defining its vision, mission, values, principles, and outcomes within the context of the attitudes, norms, beliefs, and values of the larger community. A sense of trust is critical to successful community development strategies.

Understanding Community

Understanding the community—its people, cultures, and values—provides the foundation for effective collaboration. It allows the practitioner to gain a sense of the vision the community has for itself and the underlying values of the citizenry. The practitioner will recognize the diversity of strengths and weaknesses that influence the success of the collaboration. A view of the overall strengths can be made so as not to focus on the weaknesses.

Competencies: What Are Your Strengths as a Manager?

When thinking about the competencies you need to possess as a manager, also consider the knowledge, skills, abilities, and personal characteristics needed to succeed. These can vary depending on your industry and corporate structure, but they generally involve at least some of the following:

Knowledge

Management theory	Leadership theory, organizational structures, organizational behavior, systems thinking, management information systems, business processes
Finance and accounting	Forecasting, financial reports
Economics	Knows how to interpret economic conditions of his/her region and anticipate the impact on the team.
Marketing	Knows how to identify customer groups, their tendencies, preferences, etc. Knows how to craft approaches to the different groups
Business regulations procedures	HR laws and regulations; local, regional, and and federal business regulations
Industry knowledge	Industry trends, players, developments
Company knowledge	Vision, mission, and values; policies and procedures; strategic plans, organization and structure; culture
Technical knowledge	Knowledge of the team's business processes

Skills

Problem-solving skills	Data collection, problem analysis, solution generation, decision making, program development
Interpersonal skills	Listening, speaking, writing, mentoring, coaching, conflict management, negotiation, persuasion, training, giving feedback, group facilitation
Technical skills	Basic competence in duties and tasks of direct reports

Abilities

Endurance	Able to maintain high energy over extended periods of time
Self-Awareness	Aware of own emotions, accurately assesses own strengths and weaknesses
Self-Regulation	Controls own behaviors, keeps commitments despite personal harm, able to put off immediate wants for long-term benefit, adapts to change
Empathy	Senses others' feelings, shows genuine concern for others' development
Political awareness	Sensitive to organizational politics, recognizes the political impact of alternative courses of actions
Abstract reasoning	Able to quickly grasp new concepts, thinks "out of the box," able to mentally manipulate multiple concepts simultaneously

Leadership	Able to inspire others to achieve the previously unachievable, inspires trust and confidence in others

Personal Characteristics

Learning orientation	Seeks continuous improvement, curious, constantly increasing own knowledge
Motivation	Driven by values, not deterred by personal setbacks, focuses on possibilities rather than limitations
Action orientation	Takes initiative, has a sense of urgency, decisive, willing to take risks
Integrity	Keeps promises, matches words with actions, faithful to personal and organizational values
Accountability	Holds self and others responsible for results of their actions
Team orientation	Considers others in making decisions, subverts own desires for benefit of the team, appreciates the strengths of diversity

As manager, what are you doing to maximize your talents and capabilities as a team leader?

Remember, whatever your team's particular weak spot is, my total managing system can solve it. So read on, and get ready to lead more effectively than ever.

90 Days to a High-Performance Team

PART ONE

MAKING THE TEAM WORK: GETTING IT DONE IN TEN STEPS

CHAPTER ONE

YOU'VE JUST STARTED MANAGING YOUR TEAM...NOW WHAT?

Y ou've just been hired, been promoted, or decided to take a fresh approach to managing your team. Where should you begin? From among what I refer to as the three Ps—people, processes, and priorities—choose start with your people.

Before You Start: Preplanning the Approach

Assess Your Team Members

You should have an assessment of each team member, written by a third party, ready for review. These can be past performance reviews or informal assessments written by colleagues who have worked extensively with them in the past. However, it's crucial not to let others' views and reviews of anyone on your team bias your perspective. One of the worst mistakes we can make as managers is to not give someone at least two chances to succeed, potentially three, depending on the circumstance or situation. If you can't get a third-party assessment of your team members, it's all the more important to meet with them.

Plan to Meet with Team Members

Before scheduling the team meeting—both as a team and individually—create a plan for what you will say during the meeting that includes:

1. The vision and goals you will present to your team
2. A list of your expectations of team members
3. How you will let team members know, emphatically, that *your number one job* is to support them (be sure you mean this and will deliver on it, or your credibility will vanish instantaneously)
4. An outline of your priorities for today, this week, this month, this quarter, and this year
5. Your plan for scheduling team members for one-on-one meetings (preferably within the first week), so you can convey individual performance expectations. During the team meeting, you will let them know the following:

   - They will be meeting with you one-on-one to review their performance to date.
   - At that meeting, each of them will be expected to review their performance to date, so you can understand and appreciate their perspectives.
   - You will be developing a Performance Plan in concert with them, focusing on their Top Three Performance Priorities for the next month, quarter, and year.

Create an Agenda for Your First Meeting

On the top of the agenda for your first meeting should be the team's charter. See **Table 1.1**: Agenda for Validating a Team's Charter for an example of the various elements of the charter and the estimated times for their discussion. This exercise will help you assess the needs and desires of the team, as well as possible obstacles, long-term goals, and suggested strategies for reaching them.

First Day: What Do You Say?
What Do You Hear? How Do You Respond?

Team Meeting

Now you are ready to schedule your first team meeting. During the meeting, ensure that you've covered all the essentials using **Worksheet 1.1:** Outcomes for First Team Meeting.

First Week: What Are Your Top Three Priorities?

Priority #1: Reporting Your Team Action Plan to Your Manager and Senior Management

Your first priority as manager in your first week is to convey back to senior management and to your manager (or, in some cases, the board of directors) your Team Action Plan. This is the plan you came up with on the first day using **Table 1.1:** Agenda for Validating a Team's Charter and **Worksheet 1.1:** Outcomes for First Team Meeting. If you are conducting triage, it can often be helpful to consult with a trusted managerial peer, off whom you can bounce your ideas and ask for suggestions. Enlisting someone else for advice and support is an excellent prompt toward providing the same advice and support for that colleague going forward, especially if your new position comes as a result of having changed companies or industries. This kind of manager-to-manager communication supports more cohesive team action and results moving forward. For example, when I managed at BayBank (now part of Bank of America), I was constantly consulting my manager-peers for advice, because I was new to parts of the organization and to managing a team within certain functions of the company.

TABLE 1.1 Agenda for Validating a Team's Charter

Task	Estimated Time
Send agenda, draft of team's charter, potential schedule, review schedule, and other relevant information to all participants at least one week before the meeting. Be certain that each person has all elements of the charter in front of him or her when the meeting begins.	N/A
Begin the session by introducing yourself, the agenda, and the outcomes (approval of team's charter, mission, purpose, and goals). Ask for feedback on the agenda. Make changes if necessary and announce them to the group.	15 minutes
Have the team's sponsor (usually an executive or senior leader in the organization) provide a short overview of the team and its history. Have stakeholders introduce themselves and their roles vis-à-vis the team.	30 minutes
Go through each element of the current charter—mission, purpose, and goals—one at a time. Have each participant rate each element on a scale of 1 to 5, with 5 as "completely agree" and 1 as "not agree." Ask if there are questions regarding each element. Keep a written log of comments and changes.	60 minutes
Work through each element one by one until you have reached agreement on it. You may have to go around a number of times. Use a consensus process.	1–2 hours
Review changes, modifications, or new actions for each element.	30 minutes
Discuss risks associated with the team's work and how they may be mitigated. Introduce the idea of potential conflicts of interest and resources. Briefly discuss how these might be addressed.	15–30 minutes
Discuss a preliminary schedule and how often work should be reviewed with each type of stakeholder or champion. Have a draft of this to present to the group, including agreement on the method of information sharing (e-mail, shared software, and so on). Select the simplest method. Understand each stakeholder's experience in using these technologies.	30–45 minutes
Set a follow-up schedule. Ask if there are any final comments. Distribute notes within 48 hours.	15 minutes

WORKSHEET 1.1 Outcomes for First Team Meeting

1. Team members understand the charter, mission, and scope of the team.

2. The team develops norms for team behavior and team processes:

   - How to schedule meetings; who has authority to schedule others; use of electronic scheduling or calendaring systems

   - How often voice mail and e-mail are to be answered

   - Etiquette for face-to-face meetings, audio conferences, and video conferences

   - How agendas for team meetings will be developed and distributed

   - How minutes will be taken and distributed (timing and method)

   - Who will facilitate meetings?

3. Team members understand their accountabilities and those of other team members.

   - Accountabilities of all team members are reviewed and agreed upon.

4. The team develops a plan for the use of technology, including:

   - Agreement on major type of work (parallel, sequential, or pooled sequential)

   - Technology needed given the type of work

   - How to exchange information and documents

   - Hardware and software needs of team members (e-mail, fax, telephone, video, and so on)

   - How information and documents will be stored (team Web site, shared files, or other)

   - When to mark e-mail messages and other documents "urgent," "important," or the like

   - Acquisition of new technology (for example, groupware, electronic meeting systems)

   - Training and orientation for team members in technology

   - Review of compatibility issues (MAC or PC, word-processing applications, Internet providers)

5. The team develops an external communication plan:

   - Which stakeholders, partners, champions, and others will get what information and when?

   - Which team members will coordinate with those individuals and answer questions?

6. The team determines how it will review progress:

   - Frequency of team meetings

   - Preliminary agenda for review sessions

   - Who will be required to attend

   - How meetings will be held (audio conference, video conference, and so on)

7. Team-building activities are conducted, and team norms are reviewed.

Priority #2: Meeting with Your Team

During your first week managing your team, your second priority is meeting with your team, using the guidelines presented in the first part of this chapter.

Priority #3: Meeting with Team Members One-on-One

After conducting the team meeting, you will meet with people one-on-one. If for some reason you can't meet with everyone one-on-one in your first week, be sure to schedule these meetings as soon as humanly possible. Here are some suggestions for how to get the most out of your one-on-one meetings.

1. Before meeting, let your team members know that they should come prepared to address and defend their performance to date.
2. Follow the meeting schedule you've chosen.
3. During the meetings, address the following:

   - Review their performance to date, as you understand it.
   - Listen and take notes as they offer their perspective on their performance to date.
   - Explore ways to agree on what their Performance Plan should be, going forward, using **Worksheet 1.2**: Performance Plan Template.
   - Identify the action steps (performance steps) they should follow.
   - Indicate to them, right on their Performance Plan, what steps you will be taking as a manager to support their success.

Outcomes

Team members understand what is expected of them. Job responsibilities include:

Responsibility #1:

Responsibility #2:

Responsibility #3:

Planning for Performance

Toward each responsibility, expected performance steps include:

Responsibility #1:

Performance Steps and Time Line for Accomplishing:

1.

2.

3.

Responsibility #2:

Performance Steps and Time Line for Accomplishing:

1.

2.

3.

Responsibility #3:

Performance Steps and Time Line for Accomplishing:

1.

2.

3.

Manager's Support

Toward each series of performance steps, the manager will provide the following support:

First Month: Success Against the Top Three Priorities—Next Steps

Against each of our Top Three Priorities, let's focus on what we can do during that very important first month.

1. *Managing Your Success.* You need to be as efficient as possible in managing your day, your time, and your weekly schedule, so you can succeed and be a model for your team. You may find that some suggested strategies don't work for you personally, and, as you settle into your role, you will develop your own system. But as a jumping-off point, here are some steps that have worked for me:

   - *Managing Your Day.* Before starting the day, identify your Top Three Priorities for today. What do I need to accomplish? What do I want to accomplish?
   - *Managing Your Time.* In addition to identifying your daily Top Three Priorities, group similar tasks together for completion at the same time. Help others manage their time more effectively by guiding them around what has worked for you.
   - *Managing Your Week.* At 9:00 on Monday morning, picture Friday afternoon. What did you accomplish this past week that gave you great satisfaction? Now make sure you schedule these accomplishments as tasks for this week.
   - *Managing Your Month.* Just as you did for each day and each week, list your goals and priorities. Accomplish them in bite-size daily and weekly gulps; if you have a large project you're working on, break it down into manageable pieces.

Managing Your Time

As a quick exercise in big-picture thinking, I sometimes ask my clients, "If you had an extra three hours in your week, what would you do with them?" **Exercise 1.1:** Managing Your Time accomplishes two things. First, it identifies at least one important task you consistently put off, and allows you to consider where among your goals and priorities you might be able to fit it. Otherwise, it may never get done! And second, it reminds you of all the fun things you could do if you were so well-organized that you could get your work done more efficiently and leave the office earlier. That's inspiration!

2. *Managing Your Team's Success.* Take your monthly team goals and break them down into daily and weekly goals and tasks. This gives

---

EXERCISE 1.1 Managing Your Time

What I would do with an extra three hours each week:

your team the same opportunity to succeed as you give yourself.
Be sure you are providing the promised support. Regularly ask
yourself: "How effectively am I supporting my team's success?"

3. *Managing Your Team Members' Success.* Coach people. Be
approachable. Listen to them. Provide them with constructive
feedback and support. This is not rocket science—unless, of
course, you are a rocket scientist!

Enough said. Focus on what you are doing against these Top Three
Priorities during your first month.

First 90 Days: Top Three Mantra; Managing Results; Raising the Bar

By now, you're becoming familiar with the "Top Three Mantra," one of my
favorite and most helpful concepts. It dictates that you should be speaking, thinking, and acting continually on your Top Three Priorities. For
example, as I'm getting ready to leave the house, my amused wife will often
see me walking around saying, "Jacket, keys, plastic; jacket, keys, plastic.
. . . " What I am doing is constantly stating my Top Three Priorities for
leaving the house—the items I must have to ensure my successful departure, complete and reasonably intact. At work, colleagues can often catch
me saying under my breath phrases such as, "Call, file, meeting . . . " or
"Print, review, call. . . ." What this means is that I am managing a specific
task and/or series of tasks so I can complete the tasks, projects, meetings,
or conference-call preparation successfully. When we write down our priorities and then engage in this kind of consistent "self-talk," we keep
ourselves productive. For example, though my dog Fenway is at my side
while I am writing this, I just petted him and supported his efforts at lying
down so I could stay focused on "writing, listening, writing . . . ," one of
my mantras for writing successfully.

At work, for help staying focused on your Top Three Priorities as accomplished quarterly, consider the following:

1. *Managing Your Success.* Follow these focused steps:

   - Write down your quarterly goals.
   - Schedule how you plan to accomplish your quarterly goals in bite-size daily, weekly, and monthly increments as necessary. How will you measure that, after one month, you are at least one-third of the way toward each and every one of your quarterly goals?
   - Execute your quarterly plan.
   - Review your quarterly plan at least once a month to ensure satisfactory progress (I usually do this the last Monday of each month).

2. *Managing Your Team's Success.* Try these steps on for size:

   - Write down your team's quarterly goals.
   - Communicate these goals to your team just before the new quarter starts.
   - Direct your team to schedule accomplishing the team's quarterly goals in bite-size daily, weekly, and monthly increments as necessary. Explain how you will measure that, after one month, your team is at least one-third of the way toward each and every one of its quarterly goals.
   - Execute your team's quarterly plan.
   - Review your quarterly plan at least once a month with your team to ensure satisfactory progress (consider using the last Monday of each month for this purpose).

3. *Managing Your Team Members' Success.* Follow the same steps that should now be embedded in your brain:

WORKSHEET 1.3 Outcomes for Quarterly Team Meetings

---

1. The team reviews norms for team behavior and team processes, validates, and updates them. Reviews of etiquette for audio conferences, video conferences, face-to-face meetings, and so on.

2. The progress of the team's work to date is reviewed.

3. Accountabilities are clarified, if necessary.

4. The team reviews technological issues and problems, exchanges information and documents, hardware and software needs of team members, information and document storage and access, e-mail and voice mail problems and additional technology needs, training, and orientation.

5. The team reviews progress regarding the external communication plan and verifies that information is getting to other team members, stakeholders, and champions?

6. The team assesses its work to date:
   - Progress of technical work, overlap/redundancy of roles and accountabilities
   - Availability of team members
   - Availability of information and documents
   - Access to technology
   - Access to stakeholders and other important team members

7. Additional team-building or trust-building activities are conducted, as appropriate.

8. The team reviews its current meeting effectiveness and plans for the next meeting.

- Write down your team members' quarterly goals.
- Communicate these goals to your team members just before the new quarter starts.
- Direct your team members to schedule accomplishing their quarterly goals in bite-size daily, weekly, and monthly increments as necessary. How will they know and measure that, after one month, they are at least one-third of the way toward each and every one of their quarterly goals?
- Execute your team members' quarterly plan.
- Review your team members' quarterly plan at least once a month to ensure satisfactory progress (consider having each

team member submit a Quarterly Goals Progress Report to you the last Monday of each month).

To help you plan and execute a successful quarterly team meeting, make use of **Worksheet 1.3:** Outcomes for Quarterly Team Meetings.

Implementing a New Habit

We've all heard this many times, starting with the excellent research conducted years ago by Alcoholics Anonymous and supported countless times by business leaders: It takes twenty-one straight days—or, in business terms, three consecutive weeks' working days—of consistent practice to establish a new habit. Armed with the wisdom of many others' experience, take a break and write down the next new habit you want to adopt right here. (It may feel strange, but it's really okay—as long as you own this copy of the book!)

MANAGER'S ACTION PLAN Implementing a New Habit

New habit:

Starting what day? (Tomorrow or the next day at the latest):

Scheduled into my Outlook or schedule/contact manager every day for the next three weeks' working days:

Yes (circle when done)

STOP! Don't read any further until you've:

1. Identified and written down the new habit
2. Identified the start date (tomorrow or the next day)
3. Scheduled it into Outlook or your schedule/contact manager *every day* for the next three weeks' working days

Manager's Time-Out: Human Behavior (People, Processes, and Priorities)

Now that you have "dived in" to what you are doing, give yourself a breather by thinking about the human elements that factor into managing your own behavior and managing the behavior of others. What do you know about human behavior, yours and others? Let's suggest the following:

1. We were all born with our particular genetic makeup.
2. Our interactions with other people and with our environment during the first five to six years of our lives developed our core personalities.
3. From the first stages of life and through to where we are now, we have developed our own behavioral tendencies.

John G. Geier, based on research begun by William Moulton Marston, developed an understanding of these behavioral tendencies to include: dominant, influencing, steady, and cautious. This is known to many of us as the DISC Profile System. Marston's research goal was to understand the behaviors of ordinary people and come up with a framework for interpreting mental states from behaviors.

Marston found that while basic personality traits (e.g., introversion or extroversion) do not vary significantly over time for most people, their behaviors do vary considerably from situation to situation. A person

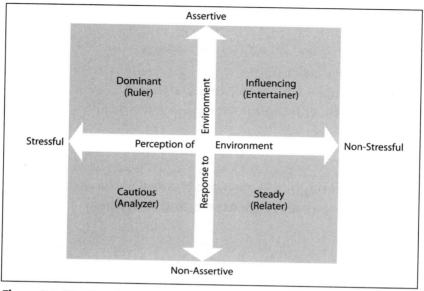

Figure 1.1 DISC Dimensions

may be very social and relaxed in one environment and very focused and driven in another. He further discovered that these behaviors could be generally explained by organizing them on two axes—one representing people's perception of their environment, and one representing their response to this perception.

One of the key implications of the DISC framework for managers is that there is no one leadership style appropriate for all employees. Different employees have different needs. The successful leader understands both individual and collective needs, and is able to respond constructively.

Consider **Figure 1.1** DISC Dimensions as a visual to help understand our own behavior and the behavior of others we are trying to manage.

Take some time to consider where each of your employees might naturally fall on the assertiveness spectrum. Then consider what you might be able to do to create an environment that brings out the best in everyone and that utilizes their innate personalities to maintain team equilibrium.

Now, let's move on to customer service . . .

CHAPTER TWO

Distinctive Customer Service: Using Under-Promising and Over-Delivering to Master Profitable Relationships

Before You Start: Products, Service, and Relationships— How Do You Distinguish Yourself, Your Team, and Your Organization?

For you, your team, and your organization to be successful, consider the following: you want to offer products that are competitive, service that is distinctive, and relationships that are premium—so much so that you will create and maintain a dynamic wherein, whenever clients or prospective clients have an itch, they will call you to scratch it. What is it about your organization's customer relationship management practices that identify you as competitive, distinctive, or premium? In every industry and every organization, increasingly competitive environments have warranted that everyone, whether they are managers, salespeople, or customer service professionals, engage in a constant-vigilance approach to customers, their problems, and solutions. We've all seen the consequences—good and bad—of information traveling faster every day, and the effect that increases in bandwidth and additional mobility are having on our collective attention spans—particularly on how effectively and frequently we communicate with customers. We also know that effective customer relationship management means gaining repeat business and referrals to new customers!

To ensure profitable relationships with customers, the questions we need to ask ourselves and prepare to ask our customers are:

- Who are our customers?
- What do our customers need? What do they want?
- How many transactions do we need to truly make a customer a "lasting" customer?
- What are the quality measures our customers use with us to decide if they are interested in a long-term relationship?
- What questions may we ask to help solve customer problems?
- How can we continue to remain customer-focused in everything we do?
- What techniques are we using that are already effective with customers?
- Why do our best customers choose to do business with us and continue doing business with us rather than the competition?
- How effectively can we repeat with everyone those behaviors that our satisfied customers value?
- How regularly are we contacting and communicating with customers?
- Are we engaged in "quality communication" with customers— that is, helping them solve their problems, rather than just checking in?
- Are we continually "present" for our customers?
- What Customer Relationship Management (CRM) technologies are we using to communicate effectively with customers and prospective customers?
- How effectively are we using these CRM technologies?
- How proactively are we evaluating prospective customers to identify their needs?
- How proactively are we engaging existing customers to identify their additional needs and anticipate their future needs?
- What are we doing to effectively close sales?

- What are we doing to master profitable customer relationships?

As you start to address your team's and your organization's customer service, ask yourself:

- Are our products competitive?
- Is our service distinct?
- Are our relationships premium?

First Day: Developing a Cogent Market Analysis for Your Enterprise and Your Customers

From the first day, for your team and your organization to succeed, you want to be clear in answering the following questions:

- Who are our customers?
- What is our ideal target market for customers?
- How effectively are we marketing our products, services, and premium relationships to and with customers?
- How are our customers finding us?
- What can we do to keep growing profitable, repeat business and relationships with our customers?

For your business to grow and keep growing, you and your team members need to be clear on who your customers are, what they want, what they need, how your organization provides your customers with what they want and what they need, and how you will keep growing your profitable customer relationships. Involving your team members in strategic thinking, engaging them in understanding and analyzing the challenges and opportunities you are facing, will help them actively participate in solving customer problems, addressing their needs, and growing your enterprise.

First Week: Approaching Customers and Prospective Customers

Before you start the first week, make sure you understand who the top 20 percent of your customers are, as they are no doubt the source for approximately 80 percent of your revenue. This is often cited as the "80-20 Rule." Who on your team is working with your top customers? How have these representatives performed? Do you have internal customers, as well? Who on your team takes care of your internal customers? Regarding both your external and internal customers, your key relationship managers are the ones driving the bulk of your business. Make these key relationship managers the "front and center" role models for your enterprise. Also consider the following steps:

1. *Partner your "less than excellent" performers with your top performers.* Your "superstars" can teach your "up-and-comers" a great deal.
2. *Make sure you have established Customer Service Performance Plans with your team members.* Give them clear expectations.
3. *What are your customer service standards?* Everyone should know them. They should be posted in a common space for everyone to understand and practice.
4. *What are your response standards?* How quickly do you return phone calls, ship orders, and respond to inquiries? As manager, make sure you are monitoring, managing, and coaching for performance against those clearly established standards.

First Month: Communicating Effectively to Grow the Enterprise

During this important first month, communicating effectively with each other and with customers is critical to your enterprise's success. That's right—communicating effectively with each other (internally) is just as important as communicating effectively with your customers, because *consistency in communication and in providing others with excellent service becomes a hallmark of what your business "says" and represents to others*. The effectiveness with which you communicate and provide excellent service to your customers, both internally and externally, leverages your company's value. *Providing consistently excellent customer satisfaction raises your own level of job satisfaction and productivity*—remember that, articulate it, and practice it every day!

First 90 Days: Using Referrals and Testimonials to Perfection

Now, when it comes to taking a 90-day approach to customer service, it is important first to understand your "sales cycles"—how long does it take for most of your transactions to close, from initial contact to signed agreement? Let's think of it in terms of our Top Three Priorities:

1. *Managing My Performance.* How effectively am I getting referrals and customer testimonials into people's hands? What steps am I taking to support team members' success?
2. *Managing My Team's Performance.* How effectively and consistently am I conveying goals and supporting team success against these goals?
3. *Managing My Team Members' Performance.* How frequently and consistently am I meeting with, observing, and coaching team members and providing support for customer service success?

Your job now is to take what you know about your sales cycles, how team members are performing, and what your best customers are telling you, and apply it to your customer service operations. Determine the specific actions that will help you meet your plan—and do it!

MANAGER'S ACTION PLAN Customer Service

Right here, right now, record your answers to these questions:

1. Who are our customers?

2. Who are our top customers?

3. Why do people, especially our top customers, do business with us instead of the competition?

4. What effective steps are we taking to address why our customers do business with us?

5. What additional steps can we take to support our customers doing business with us?

6. How do our customers find us?

7. Based on my understanding of who our customers are (especially our top customers), why do they do business with us and what we can do to continue meeting their needs? What are our business unit's and/or organization's Top Three Priorities for providing consistently excellent and improving customer service?

Customer Service Priority #1:

Customer Service Priority #2:

Customer Service Priority #3:

Now, go share these Top Three Customer Service Priorities with your team!

Manager's Time-Out: Customer Service

The most important lessons this manager and customer service provider has learned over the years are these:

1. Communicate every day with your customers. I actually try to think of them as my "clients." I define clients as people who have not only done business with you, but who also value their working relationship with you so highly that they will call you for help when they have a problem, even if it is one you cannot directly solve (you can refer them to someone who can help them directly).

2. Always keep asking them, "How may I help you?" If you ask only this one question, you are still following the most important customer service rules.

3. The next best question you can ask is, "So I can better understand, please tell me in more detail what's going on." Though there is no "question mark" there, this is a key question, a sign of your interest in them and their problem and a desire to help them solve their problem.

4. Always treat everyone as your customer, regardless of where they reside (outside or inside your organization). You never know when you are going to need their help.

Next, let's move on to communication skills. . . .
Aligning Goals Worksheet—You and Your Boss

When focused on resolving a conflict between you and your boss, it is always helpful to re-visit a shortened version of the "Goals for Roles" exercise involving you both. This will help you and your boss answer the question, "Are we on the same page?"

Suggestion: Give a blank copy of the "Goals for Roles" exercise to your boss and complete a new one yourself. Then, suggest you meet and exchange this form with them, or sit down side-by-side, exchange and/or review together, answering

What is the most important thing I can do in each of my three most important roles this week that would have the greatest positive impact?

Role: _____

Goal:

Role: _____

Goal:

Role: _____

Goal:

Time charge your goals for your most important roles each week.

CHAPTER THREE

COMMUNICATION BREAKDOWNS: WHAT TO DO AND WHAT NOT TO DO

Before You Start: What's the Problem as You See It?

To first assess how effectively we are communicating, we need to ask ourselves the following questions:

1. How is the quality of our communication helping or hurting our business?
2. What methods of communication do we use effectively?
3. What methods of communication could we be using more effectively?

You should be listing your answers to these questions so you can clearly present your perspective to your team. First, inform your team that you will be either meeting specifically to discuss workplace/department communication or incorporating this as an agenda item for your next team meeting. You should also ask them to write down the team's communication problems as they see them and bring their notes to the meeting. **Table 3.1:** Team Communication and Preferences Survey is a sample of what your memo might look like.

TABLE 3.1 Team Communication and Preferences Survey

MEMO

TO: Team

FROM: Manager

RE: Communication Methods and Preferences

It is in our best interests to support continually improving team performance. One of the ways we can support this is to communicate effectively with one another.

Please take a few moments to ponder and respond individually to these questions:

1. How do you prefer to communicate with me (your manager)? Phone, face-to-face, e-mail, perhaps a blend? Please be as specific as you can.

2. How often do we need to communicate?

3. What communication method(s) might we better utilize to facilitate our (your and my) communication? For example, would you prefer we have more phone, e-mail, and/or face-to-face contact? For whatever method(s) you cite, please indicate the frequency for the communication method(s) that you might prefer.

4. Do you have the information from me that you need to do your job?

You should also distribute a Team Member Role Assessment (see **Table 3.2**), which will help each and every team member understand, clarify, and confirm his or her team role, which will, in turn, contribute to effective communication.

TABLE 3.2 Team Member Role Assessment

Instructions: Under each statement, please check the answer that best characterizes your activities on the team.

Coordination and Collaboration

1. How often do you interface with top management at your location about the team and its progress?

   ❏ Never   ❏ Once in a while   ❏ Sometimes   ❏ Quite a bit   ❏ Continually

2. How often do you systematically report to the team about local concerns, interests, and reactions to the team's work?

   ❏ Never   ❏ Once in a while   ❏ Sometimes   ❏ Quite a bit   ❏ Continually

3. How often do you report to other team members about progress on your work or on the success of deliverables?

   ❏ Never   ❏ Once in a while   ❏ Sometimes   ❏ Quite a bit   ❏ Continually

4. How often do you gauge your actions against their impact on other team members?

   ❏ Never   ❏ Once in a while   ❏ Sometimes   ❏ Quite a bit   ❏ Continually

5. How often do you and other team members discuss the level of coordination and collaboration that is appropriate for the team?

   ❏ Never   ❏ Once in a while   ❏ Sometimes   ❏ Quite a bit   ❏ Continually

6. How often do you and your team members take the time to share learnings?

   ❏ Never   ❏ Once in a while   ❏ Sometimes   ❏ Quite a bit   ❏ Continually

Continued overleaf

TABLE 3.2 Team Member Role Assessment, *continued*

Autonomy

1. How often do you participate in activities with the team where you use specialized expertise?

   ❏ Never ❏ Once in a while ❏ Sometimes ❏ Quite a bit ❏ Continually

2. How often do you reconcile competing priorities among this team's needs, other teams' needs, and local needs?

   ❏ Never ❏ Once in a while ❏ Sometimes ❏ Quite a bit ❏ Continually

3. How often do you clarify ambiguous tasks with the team leader and/or with other team members?

   ❏ Never ❏ Once in a while ❏ Sometimes ❏ Quite a bit ❏ Continually

4. How often do you take the initiative to conduct networking and boundary-spanning activities on the team's behalf?

   ❏ Never ❏ Once in a while ❏ Sometimes ❏ Quite a bit ❏ Continually

5. How often do you assess your progress on the team in relation to your personal goals?

   ❏ Never ❏ Once in a while ❏ Sometimes ❏ Quite a bit ❏ Continually

---

Next, you should discuss your communication issues with the team, following up periodically in accordance with your agreed-upon milestones.

First Day: What Is the Problem as They See It?

Too often, team managers take a didactic or directive approach, saying something like, "These are the communication issues. This is what we're going to do to fix them." A more helpful approach is for you to follow the suggestions mentioned in the "Before" section (see **page 27**), and then incorporate this approach into your team meeting. Try these steps:

1. Present the communication issues as you see them, listing them on a whiteboard or flip chart.
2. Let others suggest additional issues and/or confirm—or disagree with—what you have written down.
3. Review the communication issues as you understand them as a team. When you give someone an opportunity to participate in helping you to understand and analyze the problem, they are highly likely remain to participate in the solution.
4. Prioritize communication issues, with the most potentially damaging problems on the top of the list, and outline suggested approaches for dealing with them, asking team members for input.
5. Develop action steps, asking everyone for their support in implementing the action steps.
6. Close the meeting positively and on time, thanking everyone for their participation during the meeting and their cooperation in helping to improve workplace/department communication.

First Week: Let's Relate, Strategize, and Implement Solutions Together—RSI in Action

In communicating effectively and in solving problems, you should consider a systematic approach of relating, strategizing, and implementing (RSI). See **Figure 3.1** RSI Model of Problem Solving.

Goals of Communicating Effectively: What We Want to Accomplish

We want to:

1. Recognize that communication is a two-way street that we all travel in order to resolve problems, make decisions, improve performance, and attain results.

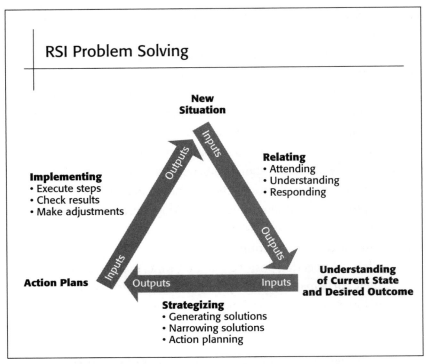

Figure 3.1 RSI Model of Problem Solving

2. Define a problem as any situation in which there is a gap between your current state and your desired state. This doesn't imply that your current state is wrong or bad, but simply that there is some other state in which you would rather be.

3. Start solving problems by *relating* to the world around you. We *attend*, or pay attention, to what is going on around us. This gives us observations, or data. We try to *understand* this data using our existing knowledge and beliefs. We then *respond* to our current state by asking ourselves, "Is there a meaningful gap between this state and the state in which I'd like to be?" If the answer is yes, we have at least an implied desired outcome.

4. When we have identified a meaningful gap, we create *strategies* for bridging it by *generating solutions* that we might use,

narrowing these solutions to those that we like best, and converting the solutions to *action plans*.

5. Once we have an action plan, we begin to *implement* it by *executing a step* in our plan, *checking the results* against our plan, and *making adjustments* to the plan as necessary. Each step creates a new situation and begins the problem-solving process anew until there is no longer a meaningful gap between our current and desired states.

First Month: Repeating and Building on Success

Continue to focus your progress in achieving your communication goals against the Top Three Priorities:

1. *Managing My Performance.* Ask yourself and others the following questions:

    - What are my communication goals?
    - When I shared these goals with my team, what was their response?
    - Are we all in agreement about what steps I need to take to communicate even more effectively?
    - How will I measure progress and success?
    - How do others say I have improved my communication effectiveness?

2. *Managing My Team's Performance.* To manage your team's performance effectively, ask:

    - What are my team's communication goals?
    - What steps does our team need to take to communicate even more effectively?

- How will we measure progress and success?
- How are we progressing with our communication as a team?

3. *Managing My Team Members' Performance.* To manage your team members' performance effectively, ask:

   - What are the team members' individual communication goals?
   - How will we measure progress and success?
   - How do team members say they have improved their communication effectiveness?
   - What do I say about how team members have improved their communication effectiveness?

First 90 Days: The 12-Week Team Communication Action Plan—It Works!

A 12-week team communication action plan starts with a team meeting using the following suggestions, and the agenda that follows (see **Worksheet 3.1**: Implementing a Team Communication Plan: Agenda).

Implementing a Team Communication Plan

Your team will benefit tremendously from a good communication plan that:

- Acts as a binding agreement. (When you tell people you're going to do something, having a communication plan or commitment in writing will force you to carry through with your efforts and you will have given others the opportunity to provide you with input).
- Assures that you will take advantage of all opportunities, including ongoing implementation

TEAM NAME: **DATE:**

GOALS

What are our team's communication goals?

1.

2.

3.

FORMAL COMMUNICATION

Team Meetings

Do we have . . .

1. Regularly scheduled team meetings?   ❏ Yes   ❏ No

   Frequency of meetings:

   Day of week: Start time:

2. Ad hoc meetings?   ❏ Yes   ❏ No

   Lead time needed to schedule a meeting:

Team Subgroup Meetings (If there are subgroups within the team, identify them and complete "1" or "2" for each subgroup.)

Do we have . . .

1. Regularly scheduled team meetings?   ❏ Yes   ❏ No

   Frequency of meetings:

   Day of week: Start time:

2. Ad hoc meetings?   ❏ Yes   ❏ No

   Lead time needed to schedule a meeting:

Continued overleaf

TEAM NAME: **DATE:**

Team Web Site

1. Will the team have a Web site?   ❑ Yes   ❑ No

2. What crucial information needs to be added to/updated on the Web site?

INFORMAL COMMUNICATION

1. How will we communicate ideas or issues that arise outside of a formal meeting?

2. How will we exchange work-related information?

3. Do we want to establish a team "chat room"? Why or why not?

- Helps keep communication focused
- Helps prevent unwanted surprises

When developing your communication plan, keep the following tips in mind:

- Set up a tracking system
- Incorporate two-way communication utilizing your local area network (LAN).
- Consider all of your audiences as "customers."
- Build in team member involvement.
- Use the plan to your advantage.
- Make sure team members understand their responsibility.
- Begin early.
- Announce public meetings and their dates and locations.
- Request volunteers for action teams.
- Acknowledge significant milestones throughout the process.
- Incorporate ongoing implementation activities.
- Distribute the communication plan to team members so everyone is "on the same page."

It's also a good idea to create a team directory, with each member's contact info, so you can get in touch with each other quickly and easily (see **Table 3.3**: Team Directory).

Equally useful is **Worksheet 3.2**: Reliability and Responsiveness Assessment, which evaluates the reliability and responsiveness of your team as a whole, and reveals areas that may need work. Also use **Table 3.4**: Matching Communication Tools to Activities to help establish the proper communication tools for different workplace activities and **Worksheet 3.3**: Communication Protocols List to list communication protocols.

Worksheet 3.4: Supporting Team Performance features some fundamental questions about how team members will support each other, both in success and failure. **Worksheet 3.5:** Evaluating the Communication Plan is a sample of a form we as managers can use to facilitate team communication.

As you have probably noticed, this 12-week communication action plan can be modified and updated on an ongoing basis, and forms the foundation for facilitating effective team communication.

EFFECTIVE LISTENING EXERCISES

As you may have gathered from this chapter, effective listening—not just for managers, but for all team members—is often the key to effective team performance. Here are a few exercises you might want to try with your team to help everyone become the best listeners they possibly can!

Exercise 1: Listening Without Speaking/Nonverbal Listening

Ask the group to form pairs. Have one person in each pair take a turn speaking for sixty seconds while the other person listens using nonverbal listening skills. Have them switch roles. Debrief after they have had a chance to be both speaker and listener. Some questions might include:

1. What was it like listening nonverbally?
2. What nonverbal listening skills did you and/or your partner use? (Write these out for everyone to see.)
3. What was it like speaking?
4. Did you feel listened to?
5. What listening skills did your partner practice particularly well?

Exercise 2: Listening Verbally and Nonverbally

Ask everyone to form groups of three. Group members will play one of three roles: Team Member, Listener, or Observer (they will not switch

TABLE 3.3 Team Directory

Name	Contact Information	Location

Reliability

Which structures, processes, and methodologies will we rely on as a team to minimize the risk of nonperformance?

Responsiveness

1. How frequently will we respond to e-mail?

2. How frequently will we respond to voice mail?

3. What system will we use for conveying urgency when sending a message?

4. How will we let each other know we're not available?

5. How will we let each other know that we're not able to respond immediately?

TABLE 3.4 Matching Communication Tools to Activities

Tool	Will Be Used for These Communication Activities
Face-to-Face	
Phone	
Data Conferencing	
Video Conferencing	
Voice Mail	
E-mail	
Team Web Site	
Other	

List what we have developed as communication protocols:

WORKSHEET 3.4 Supporting Team Performance

1. How will we give feedback to each other if there are issues?

2. How will we celebrate successes of the team or of individual members?

3. How will we evaluate the performance of the team?

WORKSHEET 3.5 Evaluating the Communication Plan

(Consider sending this as an e-mail to your team, to request their feedback.)

1. How will we, as a team, continually review this communication plan to ensure it is still relevant?

2. How often will it be reviewed and updated, if necessary?

Thank you for your ideas and contributions. We all benefit by learning from each other. We will discuss our communication plan at the next team meeting on [date] at [time].

roles). Before engaging in the role-play, be sure that everyone has reviewed the skills essential for active listening, summarized in **Worksheet 3.6:** Active Listening Skills Checklist.

Ask the person who is playing the role of "Team Member" to approach the person who is playing "Listener" with a work-related challenge that he or she is currently experiencing. The "Team Member" should preface the request with his or her frustration: "Please listen; I've tried to tell about half a dozen others about this and no one will listen."

The person who is playing "Listener" should do his or her best to follow the active listening skills laid out in Worksheet 3.6, which the person who is playing "Observer" will use to record his or her observations.

Give each group five to ten minutes to role-play; return everyone to one group for large group discussion. The questions you might ask include:

1. What listening skills did the Listener practice well?
2. What might the Listener have done differently?

To test your own listening skills, you can use the checklist in Worksheet 3.6.

Constructive Feedback Exercise

As all good managers know, constructive feedback goes hand-in-hand with active listening. This is the kind of input that will inspire your team members to succeed, rather than feeling criticized. Here is an exercise you can use with your team to ensure that constructive feedback is the only kind being offered.

Review **Worksheet 3.7:** Constructive Feedback Skills Checklist. Using this as a guide, identify a team member (or team members) you wish to approach. Next, contemplate how you would approach the team member, and what two compliments you would offer before sharing a suggestion for something you would like this person to do differently. Then, approach the individual and engage him or her.

WORKSHEET 3.6 Active Listening Skills Checklist

1. Open the conversation positively:

   ❑ Acknowledge and set the other at ease.

   ❑ Ask for specifics about what's going on and his/her feelings about it.

2. Focus on the other person:

   ❑ Use mirroring and paraphrasing.

   ❑ Show empathy and positive regard.

   ❑ Clarify what you don't understand.

   ❑ Accept his/her perceptions as real for him/her.

   ❑ Pay attention to his/her nonverbals.

   ❑ Don't generalize.

3. Explore the person's need:

   ❑ Ask open-ended questions.

   ❑ Clarify your understanding of what he/she is saying.

   ❑ Avoid jumping to a solution or giving advice.

   ❑ Ask what he/she specifically wants from you.

   ❑ Probe for interests behind positions, issues behind issues.

4. Summarize your understanding:

   ❑ Reflect back your understanding of the situation.

   ❑ Seek mutual consent to move forward.

(What's next for you? What's next for me?)

WORKSHEET 3.7 Constructive Feedback Skills Checklist

1. State your case:

   ❑ State your purpose/intentions and reservations clearly.

   ❑ Describe other's specific behaviors, with examples.

   ❑ Express feelings about other's behavior.

   ❑ Make "I" or "we" statements, not judging or evaluating other person.

2. Exchange information, understand perceptions:

   ❑ Ask for the other's perspective/position/perception.

   ❑ Listen, and pay attention to body language.

   ❑ Differentiate your and his/her positions and intentions.

   ❑ Check for accurate listening and understanding.

   ❑ Accept his/her emotions as is, without devaluing or negating them.

3. Seek solutions:

   ❑ Solicit his/her preferred solution.

   ❑ Request specific behavior changes.

   ❑ Describe the benefits and/or consequences of change.

4. Close the conversation:

   ❑ Verify the agreement reached and follow-up required.

   ❑ State what you have learned from the conversation.

   ❑ Express appreciation.

An additional suggestion: If you sense during and/or at the conclusion of the interaction with the team member that your advice was not well received, ask the team member to complete the Constructive Feedback Skills Checklist with you. The team member will be critiquing you. Remember, the more effectively you can model the behavior you wish team members to adopt (receiving constructive feedback well), the greater the likelihood they will better receive you this time and in the future.

Manager's Time-Out: Communication

Personal experience and close observation have taught this manager that the four most important communication skills managers need to possess and use every day are:

1. Listening effectively and actively, clarifying and confirming what you hear
2. Giving and receiving constructive feedback
3. Resolving conflicts
4. Coaching employees, both the best and the weakest

Some useful steps to take regarding these four communication skills include:

Listening

1. Use your two ears to listen twice as much as you speak.
2. Take notes.
3. Reflect a person's mood, tone, and words back to him or her.
4. Ask questions continuously.

Giving Constructive Feedback

1. Establish the ground rules for constructive feedback as indicated in **Worksheet 3.7**: Constructive Feedback Skills Checklist.
2. Give as good as you get; receive constructive feedback just as you would want others to receive it—openly!
3. As a manager, let the person to whom you are providing constructive feedback know that:

   - "I am here to support you."
   - "I'm open to hearing what I can do to support your success."
   - "These are the steps I will take to support your success."

4. By voicing your action plan, you are modeling for others to do the same.

Resolving Conflicts

1. Understand that resistance is a part of human behavior; it is neither good nor bad, just a part of people's defense mechanisms (people feel that they, or some aspect of their values and belief systems, are being threatened).
2. Do your best to understand the resistance.
3. Respond to the resistance by asking, "What can we do to resolve this?"
4. Find at least one area of agreement; when you do so, you have established a foundation for building a solution.
5. Plan action.
6. Implement action.

Coaching

1. Be as approachable as possible; let your team members know when you are generally available to speak with them.
2. If you are otherwise occupied, give people an opportunity to access you (through Outlook or other form of scheduling software).
3. Promise confidentiality in all but extenuating circumstances.
4. Focus first on the problem to ensure that you share the same understanding; then, start toward a solution.
5. Emphasize that all suggestions are geared toward helping the employee improve his or her performance.

In the next chapter, we will look at strategies for facilitating change.

CHAPTER FOUR

Facilitating Change: How to Get the "Ain't It Awfuls" on Your and Your Team's Side

Before You Start: Ain't It Awful? Clarifying and Confirming for Yourself What the Top Anticipated Changes Are

A long time ago, John Breedlove, one of my managers at Prudential, introduced me to the concept of the "Ain't It Awful" mentality. Every Friday morning, John would observe the agents from our office commiserating in the coffee shop on the first floor of our building. This commiserating, occurring immediately after people received their weekly paychecks (which were based on performance), would prompt John to say, "Oh, brother. Look at them. It's the weekly meeting of the 'Ain't It Awful' Club." What John was referring to—and capturing quite effectively—was the mentality and response some people have to disappointment or failure, which is to say, "Woe is me." Of course, the more constructive approach is to say, "Oh, well. That stunk. So what steps am I taking to improve my lot?"

Change comes differently and is responded to differently by each team leader and team. There is no one surefire way to approach and respond to change. With that in mind, based on experience, please also consider the following steps to approaching and responding to change, as introduced in Chapter 3 when we addressed communication and our team communication plan.

Before gathering your team, it's important that you have your own thoughts straight. Here are the steps you need to take:

1. Determine and list what you consider the top anticipated change(s) to be.
2. Develop a Meeting Agenda to discuss the change(s) to be implemented.
3. Before meeting and discussing with your team, develop a plan for approaching, incorporating, and implementing the change (your Change Implementation Plan).
4. Call a team meeting, asking people to bring their "Implementing Change Thinking Caps" to the meeting, and warn them they will be doing some brainstorming.

This leads us to . . .

First Day: Communicating Anticipated Changes to Your Team; Gaining Their Input

Meet with your team, following the suggested change agenda in **Table 4.1: Team Meeting Change Agenda** (which should look familiar).

First Week: The Team Approach to Addressing Change Priority #1—Implementing Action Plans

This is simpler than it may sound, if done correctly. Have the team members report in a brief meeting (thirty minutes or less) their progress against the one-week implementation plan. Chart success; make adjustments as necessary.

TIPS FOR COMMUNICATING CHANGE

- Ask people for their opinion before you implement change.

- Be so thoroughly familiar with what you are communicating that you can summarize it in a short sentence.

- Explain the change in language that people understand.

- Explain the change in terms of how it will affect them first, then how it will affect the team and your organization.

- Anticipate how people will react, the questions they'll raise, and the issues that may result.

- Design your communication to answer those concerns immediately.

- Keep your personal key communicators up-to-date regularly.

- Expect the change to generate a corps of resisters and appreciate them.

- In addition to encouraging them to participate in the implementation of the change, listen to what they have to say.

- Solicit ideas that will strengthen what you want to do.

- Identify the people on your team who you can come to for advice regarding new ideas.

- Be direct in stating the change and explaining the rationale for the change in relation to the overall goals you wish to achieve.

- Keep communicating about the change after it has been made. Recognize and celebrate its successful implementation.

First Month: Team Results Against Top Three Team Goals; Weekly Review, Charting Progress, Facilitating Results

Same idea, only over one month: Chart progress against monthly implementation goals; make adjustments as necessary.

TABLE 4.1 Team Meeting Change Agenda

1. Distribute copies of the Meeting Agenda.

2. Distribute copies of your write-up about the soon-to-be-implemented change(s), along with your Change Implementation Plan.

3. Ask people for their responses.

4. Review the Change Implementation Plan together, asking people to write down their questions and feedback, and be prepared to discuss them when you are finished reading the plan.

5. Unless someone makes a suggestion that radically alters the Change Implementation Plan, schedule its implementation, focusing on the following milestones:

   - What will we accomplish in the first week?
   - What will we accomplish in the first month?
   - What will we accomplish in the first 90 days?

6. Thank people for their participation.

7. End the meeting on time and on message (so long as you're sure that people know their "marching orders").

8. Have meeting notes/minutes distributed within twenty-four hours.

First 90 Days: How'd We Do Against Our Top Three? Recognizing and Building on Success

When it comes to a quarterly review meeting, to assess our success at implementing a change or changes, let us prepare everyone at that first monthly meeting as follows:

1. Schedule the quarterly meeting to assess change implementation success.

2. Inform team members that everyone will be held accountable for implementing their part of the plan.

TABLE 4.2 Team Meeting Change Implementation Quarterly Review

1. Distribute copies of the Meeting Agenda.
2. Have team members present their Change Implementation Quarterly Progress Reports, submitting a copy to you.
3. After everyone has presented, give your review back to the team and ask for their reactions, questions, and input, reviewing:

   - What did we accomplish in the first week?
   - What did we accomplish in the first month?
   - What did we accomplish in the first 90 days?

4. Thank people for their participation.
5. End the meeting on time and on message.
6. Have meeting notes/minutes distributed within twenty-four hours.

---

3. Also inform team members that if they are experiencing any difficulty making proportionate progress toward achieving the goals, they should inform you immediately of any difficulty so adjustments can be made midstream.
4. Inform team members that they will be expected to present a Change Implementation Quarterly Progress Report (reviewing the Change Implementation Plan) at the quarterly review meeting.
5. Conduct the quarterly review meeting following the suggested agenda in **Table 4.2**: Team Meeting Change Implementation Quarterly Review.

Manager's Time-Out: Facilitating Change

I learned a long time ago that, as managers, we need to understand quite a bit about our working relationships with our direct reports to predict how they will react to change. Let's take a look at a few of these understandings.

MANAGER'S ACTION PLAN: Facilitating Change

Right here, right now, record your answers to these questions:

    1. What are our Top Three Change Priorities?

        Change Priority #1:

        Change Priority #2:

        Change Priority #3:

Now, go share these Top Three Change Priorities with your team!

Front-Line Manager Roles

Every day, front-line managers assume a variety of roles as they interact with other people. A role is a character that the manager assumes in a particular situation, much like an actor plays a role in a film. Here are some typical managerial roles:

COACH: Develops game plans and calls plays; makes assignments; encourages team members; assesses strengths and developmental needs; builds individual and team strengths by training; allows members to practice skills; gives feedback.

TEAM CAPTAIN: Uses leadership and communication skills to build teams and hold them together; inspires confidence; communicates the vision, mission, and goals of the enterprise to team members; guides teams in development of set objectives; helps members understand the positions they play; seeks participation in team projects; openly confronts conflicts.

CHEERLEADER: Encourages team members to excel; shows and builds confidence in abilities of team members; generates enthusiasm and support for team projects both with the immediate group and from the organization as a whole.

REPORTER: Communicates information within the team; promotes the team to others.

FORTUNE TELLER: Projects trends; decides or recommends best course of action based on these predictions.

POLITICAL ANALYST: Analyzes the current politics of the enterprise and develops strategies accordingly.

COUNSELOR: Listens to employee problems; helps employees develop solutions.

PARENT: Supports and nurtures employees.

REFEREE: Calls time-out during conflicts; seeks resolution; determines penalties.

NEGOTIATOR: Brokers among people with different views; negotiates for resources.

GLADIATOR: Battles to gain support or resources; fights to protect the team or project.

HUNTER: Openly seeks new projects and sources of work for the team.

RESOURCE ALLOCATOR: Determines or recommends how the team's resources will be used.

SPOKESPERSON: Represents the organization at professional, civic, or other meetings.

DETECTIVE: Identifies problems, determines causes, and develops solutions.

When striving to effectively facilitate and implement change, you need to be mindful that you are being looked up to as a role model, and therefore are expected to embody a number of these roles. The effectiveness with which you conduct yourself as a manager in these roles and the degree to which you accept and facilitate change is directly proportionate to how effectively team members will accept and facilitate change.

Next . . . what about "troublemakers"?

CHAPTER FIVE

RIDDING YOURSELF OF THAT "ONE LITTLE TROUBLEMAKER" LEGALLY AND ETHICALLY—IN FIVE EASY STEPS

Before You Start: Who Is the Problem?
What Approaches Have We Tried?
What Worked and What Didn't?

Think about it: one troublemaker on your team can cause myriad problems, not the least of which is the deterioration of staff morale. Start by asking yourself the following questions:

1. If we have one, who is "the problem"?
2. What specific behavior have we witnessed that defines "the problem"? (List any and all specific behaviors.)
3. What approaches have we tried (if any)?
4. What has worked?
5. What hasn't?

Next, assuming that you do have an individual in mind, prepare for a one-on-one meeting, which follows these steps:

First Day: Privately Inviting the Troublemaker into a Collaborative, Problem-Solving Conversation

1. Before meeting, review what you have written in response to the questions above.
2. Contact the individual and schedule a regular performance meeting with him or her.
3. Review **Worksheet 5.1**: Constructive Feedback Skills Checklist.
4. Manage the meeting by reviewing with the "troublemaker" your responses to Questions 2 through 5 from the "Before" section on **page 57**.
5. Ask the individual for his or her response, taking exacting notes (remember, you will want to read back your notes and get his or her feedback before finishing the meeting).
6. Read back your notes, asking for feedback.
7. Offer your own suggested (and written) next steps, as you are now taking the initiative to direct the individual in the framework of "change these behaviors or be gone."
8. Plan your action steps and implementation schedule.
9. Close the conversation positively, with a forward-looking tone.

To aid in your goal of a productive conversation in this meeting, revisit Worksheet 5.1.

There needs to be an action plan that addresses which behaviors will change within:

- One week—What steps will the individual take? How will you measure progress?
- One month—What steps will the individual take? How will you measure progress?

You need to inform the individual of the severity of the situation and the accountability and consequences conditioned upon his or her changing these behaviors swiftly.

WORKSHEET 5.1 Constructive Feedback Skills Checklist

1. State your case:

   ❑   State your purpose/intentions and reservations clearly.

   ❑   Describe other's specific behaviors, with examples.

   ❑   Express feelings about other's behavior.

   ❑   Make "I" or "we" statements, not judging or evaluating other person.

2. Exchange information, understand perceptions:

   ❑   Ask for the other's perspective/position/perception.

   ❑   Listen, and pay attention to body language.

   ❑   Differentiate your and his/her positions and intentions.

   ❑   Check for accurate listening and understanding.

   ❑   Accept his/her emotions as is, without devaluing or negating them.

3. Seek solutions:

   ❑   Solicit his/her preferred solution.

   ❑   Request specific behavior changes.

   ❑   Describe benefits and/or consequences of change.

4. Close the conversation:

   ❑   Verify agreement reached and follow-up required.

   ❑   State what you have learned from the conversation.

   ❑   Express appreciation.

First Week: Progress Against Action Plan from Troublemaker and Troubled Team

Meet with the individual approximately one week after your first meeting. Review his or her progress against the one-week objectives. If this person has failed to meet any of the one-week objectives, write a warning and give him or her a copy to sign. But keep in mind that in virtually all jurisdictions, the individual is within his or her rights to refuse to sign.

First Month: Reviewing Performance; Clarifying and Confirming Salvageability; Warnings?

Meet with the individual approximately one month after your first meeting. Review his or her progress against the one-month objectives. If this person has failed to meet any of the one-month objectives, write a warning and give him or her a copy to sign.

After one month, the person should have made the necessary adjustments. Be sure to commend and congratulate the individual for any adjustments he or she has made. At the same time, as a manager, if there are any unresolved issues, you have to make a decision now regarding whether this person's performance can be salvaged and the impact his or her behavior is having on other team members, on the team, and on productivity. Has the person made sufficient progress? As the NFL commercial used to say, "You make the call!"

If there are any specific issues where the individual may be able to continue making progress over the next four to eight weeks, list them, review them with the individual, and have him or her review and sign these conditions. In some cases, you can justify retaining an individual who still has progress to make after one month; after all, it takes time to make meaningful change. But for the sake of efficiency and your own sanity, keep your attempts to remedy the person's behavior relatively short-term, and always measurable and accountable.

First 90 Days: Still with Us or Gone? Progress Against Action Plans: Cut or Contributing?

For anyone you have decided to keep beyond thirty days who still needs to improve performance, the individual needs to demonstrate consistent progress or it is time to schedule a meeting with Human Resources. Ask yourself, "Is this person still contributing sufficiently to justify our keeping them?" You're the manager; it's your decision.

MANAGER'S ACTION PLAN Dealing with the Troublemaker

Right here, right now, record your answers to these questions:

1. What value does this person add to our organization/department?

2. What does this person do (specific behaviors are a must!) to detract from our team's performance?

3. What will it cost me to remove this person from our function/organization?

4. Is it worth it?

Based on your answers, take appropriate action—today. Don't wait; that will only cost you more.

Manager's Time-Out: Managing Performance While Dealing with the Troublemaker

Managing is a complex function in any organization and requires a diverse set of competencies. Below is a generic set of duties and competencies that apply to managers anywhere. The amount of time any given manager spends on any duty depends on a number of factors—organizational level, function, size of team, and so on. Sometimes, when dealing with a problem employee, we let other things fall by the wayside. But all managers should be spending some time, even if it's less than usual, on each of these duties.

EXTERNAL AWARENESS: Identifying and analyzing industry, regional, and company developments that have the potential to affect the team.

INTERPRETATION: Keeping subordinates informed about key company and team policies, priorities, issues, and trends and how these are to be incorporated in team activities and products.

REPRESENTATION: Presenting, explaining, selling, and defending the team's activities to supervisors, others in the company, clients, and/or community organizations.

COORDINATION: Performing liaison functions and integrating team activities with the activities of other offices or product lines.

STRATEGIC PLANNING: Developing and deciding upon longer-term goals, objectives, and priorities; and developing and deciding among alternative courses of action.

TACTICAL PLANNING: Converting plans to actions by setting short-term objectives and priorities; scheduling/sequencing activities; and establishing effectiveness and efficiency standards/guidelines.

BUDGETING: Preparing, justifying, and/or administering the team's budget.

MATERIAL RESOURCE ALLOCATION: Assuring the availability of adequate supplies, equipment, facilities; overseeing procurement/contracting activities; and/or overseeing logistical operations.

HUMAN RESOURCE MANAGEMENT: Projecting the number and types of staff needed by the team, and using various personnel management system components (e.g., recruitment, selection, promotion, performance appraisal) in managing the team.

SUPERVISING: Providing day-to-day guidance and oversight of subordinates (e.g., work assignments, consultation, and so on); and actively working to promote and recognize performance.

TEAM PERFORMANCE MANAGEMENT: Keeping up-to-date on the overall status of activities in the team, identifying problem areas, and taking corrective actions (e.g., rescheduling, reallocating resources, and so on).

PROGRAM EVALUATION: Critically assessing the degree to which program/project goals are achieved and overall effectiveness/efficiency of team operations, to identify means for improving team performance.

When we are thinking about how we are going to deal with a troublemaker, how does the time we are devoting to that problem take away from the time, thought, and energy we should be applying to these duties and responsibilities? Think about it, and take corrective action—today.

Now, what about that "boss from hell"?

CHAPTER SIX

"The Boss from Hell"— Help Is on the Way!

Before You Start: Discussing with Trusted Others, Seeking Advice

Speaking as someone who has had two bosses with whom I had great difficulty getting along—with the understanding that I found a way to peacefully coexist with one and had to leave the other—let us take a constructive approach to dealing with the so-called "boss from hell."

First, try sitting down with at least one trusted colleague and ask this person for his or her understanding and advice. I'm guessing there is at least one person in your office in whom you can confide. Try to choose someone who seems even-tempered and gets along well with others. Ask this colleague for advice and seek to implement his or her suggestions (if they seem appropriate).

First Day: Approaching the Boss Collaboratively

If there is no one at work in whom you can confide, ask yourself the following questions:

1. What have I written down on my list of "objectionable behaviors"?
2. Have I met with this individual privately to discuss the difficulty of our working relationship?

3. If so, what was this person's response?
4. If not, how soon can I schedule a meeting with this individual?
5. Is this working relationship worth salvaging? In other words, do I want this job/this opportunity/to work in this organization enough to remain?

If you answered no to the last question, plan your exit and look for other opportunities. If you answered yes to the last question, consider the following steps:

1. If you haven't already met with this person, do so as soon as possible. Follow the steps in **Worksheet 6.1**: Resolving Conflicts Skills Checklist.
2. If you have already met with the individual, and were unable to resolve anything, go to Human Resources and discuss the matter privately. Ask for their help and suggestions.

First Week: That Important Conversation: Progress or "Punt"?

If you are having that direct conversation, please, for your own benefit, follow the **Worksheet 6.1**: Resolving Conflicts Skills Checklist. Take notes. Be sure that before you leave that meeting, you have a plan that will allow you both to peacefully coexist. If you don't, and wish to remain, discuss your issue with someone in Human Resources. One of their suggestions will probably be to look for other opportunities internally, so it might make sense to look at internal postings before that meeting and determine if any of them might be of interest.

Worksheet 6.1 Resolving Conflicts Skills Checklist

Approach Resistance:

- ❑ Keep communication lines open
- ❑ Don't rush the process
- ❑ Beware of the resistance (the reactions) within yourself
- ❑ Ask what you can learn from it
- ❑ Seek mutual gain

Dealing with Resistance:

- ❑ Look for behavioral clues
- ❑ Trust your instincts / visceral responses
- ❑ Maintain your focus / objectives
- ❑ Stay calm / treat resistors with respect
- ❑ Embrace / give voice to the resistance
- ❑ Let others respond
- ❑ Seek themes, metaphors, new possibilities in the resistance

State Your Case:

- ❑ State your purpose/intentions and reservations clearly
- ❑ Describe other's specific behaviors, with examples
- ❑ Express feelings about other's behavior
- ❑ Make "I" or "we" statements, not judging or evaluating the other person

Exchanging Information, Understanding Perceptions:

- ❑ Ask for the other person's perspective/position/perception
- ❑ Listening, and paying attention to body language
- ❑ Differentiate your and their positions and intentions
- ❑ Check for accurate listening and understanding
- ❑ Accept their emotions as is, without devaluing or negating them

Finding Areas of Agreement / Seeking Solutions:

- ❑ Where can we agree?

continued overleaf

Worksheet 6.1 Resolving Conflicts Skills Checklist, *continued*

- ❏ Solicit their preferred solution
- ❏ Request specific behavior changes
- ❏ Describe benefits and/or consequences of change

Closing the Conversation:

- ❏ Verify agreement reached and follow-up required
- ❏ State what you have learned from the conversation
- ❏ Express appreciation

First Month: What Has Improved and What Hasn't?

Okay, now it is time to list out the pros and cons of remaining in the organization, using two separate columns on one piece of paper. Discuss your findings with a trusted other, perhaps a colleague or your spouse. Make sure you emerge with a plan following one of these three paths:

1. Continue in the same organization in the same department.
2. Continue in the same organization in a different department.
3. Work somewhere else.

First 90 Days: Reviewing Working Relationship Progress; Charting Next Steps

Okay, if you've remained for ninety days, it should mean you've found a way to peacefully coexist. Let's look at the two possibilities at this point:

1. You've found a way to peacefully coexist. What has improved? Has anything not improved? If nothing has improved, it is imperative you revisit this issue with your boss, once again using the Resolving Conflicts Skills Checklist.

2. Things have improved somewhat, enough to keep you there, but you have lingering concerns. Try one more meeting. If nothing changes, discuss with Human Resources, making sure to look for remedies and/or other opportunities in your organization before pursuing outside opportunities.

Above and beyond all, don't despair. You are certainly not the first person who has had difficulty getting along with a boss. Discuss with your spouse or trusted other. Ask for and consider the advice you are given. Take constructive steps that will help you stop feeling miserable, even if they don't solve the problem right away. You'll find great relief just in breaking your paralysis.

Manager's Time-Out: Improving Your Working Relationships Not Just with Your Boss, but with Everyone

When looking to improve your working relationships, it is very important to keep in mind that you are both a manager and a leader. Let's deepen our understanding of leading and managing.

What is the difference between leadership and management? In much of recent business literature, there has been a trend toward leadership and away from management. This is in response to management bureaucracies that flourished during the "scientific management" revolution. The emphasis on controlling performance by taking decision making out of the hands of employees left many employees feeling disconnected from their work and indifferent toward their employers. Leadership, defined as setting an inspiring vision and then letting employees manage their own work, was seen as the cure.

To help you and the boss with whom you are having a conflict, why not try a "check-in" with them to ensure your goals are aligned? To achieve this goal, use "**Worksheet 6.2** Aligning Goals—You and Your Boss" that follows.

Worksheet 6.2 Aligning Goals—You and Your Boss

When focused on resolving a conflict between you and your boss, it is always helpful to revisit a shortened version of the "Goals for Roles" exercise involving you both. This will help you and your boss answer the question, "Are we on the same page?"

Suggestion: Give a blank copy of the "Goals for Roles" exercise to your boss and complete a new one yourself. Then, suggest you meet and exchange this form with him or her, or sit down side-by-side, exchange and/or review together, answering What is the most important thing I can do in each of my three most important roles this week that would have the greatest positive impact?

Role: _____

Goal: _____

Role: _____

Goal: _____

Role: _____

Goal: _____

Time charge your goals for your most important roles each week.

Right here, right now, record your answers to these questions:

1. What is working about my relationship with my boss?

2. What could work better in our relationship?

3. What steps do I want my boss to take to improve our working relationship?

4. What steps can I take to improve our working relationship?

Now, schedule that meeting with your boss to try and make things better—today.

Many businesses in high-tech and services have recently, however, begun to see the reverse syndrome. Dot-coms have had inspiring visions, but employees, while technically proficient, often haven't known how to turn the inspiring vision into solid results. The resulting leadership-without-management paradigm has been equally unsuccessful.

Managing is what managers do—planning, hiring, organizing work, reviewing performance, and so on. Leadership is how they do it—the ways in which managers engage with employees to get the performance they want.

Directive vs. Participative Leadership

Table 6.1: Attitudes Toward Work describes two theories created by organizational theorist Douglas McGregor. Theory X represents what he saw as traditional assumptions about people's attitudes toward work. Theory Y is based on his subsequent observations and research.

Theory X led to a very directive form of leadership, in which the manager retained all control and rarely relinquished any. The shift in thought to Theory Y led to a much more participative approach to leadership-shared vision, employee involvement, and so forth. The secret to high-performance supervision lies in knowing what mix of directive and participative leadership to use and when.

When we are looking to manage working relationships, we need to keep these distinctions in their proper context. Let's remember, we're trying to solve problems as managers, which will help our team improve performance!

As managers and as team leaders, we have a single overarching function—to accomplish company goals by enabling others. As a human being, you are a natural problem solver. You've risen to the level of manager by successfully and independently solving problems. To be the best possible manager, you must grow in your ability to solve problems interdependently. Management exists because of the belief that one person

TABLE 6.1 Attitudes Toward Work

Theory "X"	Theory "Y"
• People dislike work	• Work is natural
• People want direction	• Ability is uniformly distributed
• People want no responsibility	• People seek responsibility
• People value security above all	• People like to direct their own efforts

enabling the work of several others is more effective than each trying to work separately.

As an individual contributor, you solved problems independently by analyzing a situation to describe its current state, envisioning a desired state, generating a strategy for moving toward the desired state, and implementing that strategy. You were effective because you had strong knowledge and skills in your technical field, be it programming, sales, R&D, and so on. As a manager you will continue to use those problem-solving skills, but you must add a new set of knowledge and skills in a new field—the field of Human Performance.

We all solve problems when we have to, but why are some more adept at it than others? There are a number of answers, but one stands out. People who use a conscious, systematic approach to solving problems are consistently more successful than those who do not. There are also people with natural brilliance who can solve problems in their particular fields intuitively, but their success is often limited to their specialties. On an everyday basis, it is the person who employs a conscious process, with rigor and discipline, who succeeds consistently at achieving their goals.

So, ask yourself this . . . . What steps am I taking today to achieve my goals?

Next: What if your team is clashing with another team?

CHAPTER SEVEN

Your Team Is Clashing with Another Team—Getting Everyone on the Same Page

Before You Start: Writing Down Your "Clash Assessment"

If your team is clashing with another team, take some notes in response to these questions:

1. In my best judgment, what is the reason(s) our teams are in conflict? (Note: Most often, teams clash due to competition for the same resources.)
2. Are any of the reasons regarding "lack of trust"? (If so, stay tuned for how to conduct a Team Trust Audit [**Worksheet 7.1**].)
3. If trust is not involved, continue writing notes and start ranking, in order of importance, what you understand as the key reasons the two teams are in conflict.

Either way, when two teams are in conflict, it is not a bad idea to conduct a Team Trust Audit.

Team Trust Audit

A Team Trust Audit is a useful way to obtain real-time and/or ongoing feedback about actions that are important to the team and to any teams that are in conflict. After the team has determined which items from the Team Trust Audit are meaningful to its members, questionnaire items can be constructed that provide the team and its leader with feedback on how the team is doing. The questionnaire can be put into an e-mail format and administered on a regular basis. The results serve as a point of departure for the team members to debrief how they are performing in each trust area.

New items can be added as the team matures and as new issues arise. Rotating the responsibility for summarizing results and leading the team's debriefing and action-planning session can give everyone a sense of participation in building trust. When debriefing, use an agenda that everyone has agreed upon and be certain that all responses remain anonymous and that all items are thoroughly discussed and resolved. No item or response is too minute or unimportant to be addressed.

If debriefing sessions are conducted by audio conference or video-conference, schedule at least two hours. If necessary, obtain the help of a professional meeting facilitator. Always find a way to follow up on actions in a timely manner.

A list of some of the elements found in a standard Team Trust Audit is shown in **Worksheet 7.1,** which correspond to the three factors of trust: performance and competence, integrity, and concern for the well-being of others. It is not necessary to have a large number of items in your questionnaire. Instead, pay attention to creating a questionnaire that is meaningful, easy to respond to, anonymous, and focused on your team's unique concerns and issues.

WORKSHEET 7.1 Team Trust Audit

TRUST FACTORS	EXAMPLES	MANAGER ACTIONS, TEAM MEMBER ACTIONS
Performance and Competence *Develop and display competence.*	Focus on individual and team results.	
	Keep current in your technical area of expertise.	
	Continue reading and learning about new skills, processes, approaches, and so on.	
	Be open to new ideas and methods.	
	Be able to say, "I don't know."	
	Allow others to be experts.	
	Foster expertise and sharing on the team—for example, set an agenda item for sharing learnings and establish a project Web page to share learnings.	
Follow through on commitments and show results.	Keep a log of commitments and make them visible to the team through e-mail or another means. Have a method to ensure follow-through.	
	Keep promises even if circumstances have changed.	
	Keep your commitments in cost, schedule, and technical areas. Inform team members well in advance if you will be late in any area	

Continued overleaf

WORKSHEET 7.1 Team Trust Audit, *continued*

TRUST FACTORS	EXAMPLES	MANAGER ACTIONS, TEAM MEMBER ACTIONS
Integrity *Ensure that your actions are consistent with your words.*	Align your behaviors at meetings, during reviews, and at other critical times to the values and expectations you want to promote within the team.	
	Have team members you trust watch you and give you feedback on the consistency of your words and actions.	
	Conduct regular trust audits.	
	If your actions are not consistent, explain why to your team members.	
Stand up for your convictions; display integrity.	Do the right thing in the best interest of the team or its members.	
	Be able to say, "I don't agree" to those above you.	
	Speak up for what you believe in with the team and with management.	
	Continue to do the right thing, even in a crisis or firefighting mode.	
	When appropriate, openly discuss your work-related convictions and values with team members and with management. Have an agenda item about this in team meetings.	

WORKSHEET 7.1 Team Trust Audit, *continued*

TRUST FACTORS	EXAMPLES	MANAGER ACTIONS, TEAM MEMBER ACTIONS
Stand behind the team and its people.	Keep up-to-date so that you can catch problems before you have to defend the team or any of its members.	
	Always investigate problems with the team before commenting to others about possible reasons for them.	
	Never speak negatively about the team to others.	
Communicate and keep everyone informed about progress.	Hold a regular audio conference, videoconference, or other meeting once a week and have an agenda that covers bad as well as good news.	
	Don't forget people in remote locations and extended team members.	
	Post information and decisions so that everyone has access to them.	
	Ensure that everyone receives information in a timely manner. Use multiple, synchronous, asynchronous, and redundant communication methods.	

Continued overleaf

WORKSHEET 7.1 Team Trust Audit, *continued*

TRUST FACTORS	EXAMPLES	MANAGER ACTIONS, TEAM MEMBER ACTIONS
Show both sides of an issue.	Formally present both the pros and cons of issues.	
	Post them on a Web site for the team members to read.	
	Create an environment for and schedule time for discussion and debate in team sessions. Start a chat room or other means for asynchronous discussions.	
Concern for Well-Being of Others		
Help team members with transitions.	Have standard processes for selection, rewards, assignments, and sharing of information that do not favor certain people, functions, cultures, organizations, or locations.	
	Rotate the "good" and "bad" team jobs.	
	Have standard processes for selection, rewards, assignments, and sharing of information that do not favor certain people, functions, cultures, organizations, or locations.	
	Help team members to transition off the team and to new assignments.	

WORKSHEET 7.1 Team Trust Audit, *continued*

TRUST FACTORS	EXAMPLES	MANAGER ACTIONS, TEAM MEMBER ACTIONS
	Assign partners to new team members for orientation and reassignment.	
Be aware of your impact on others.	Be aware that people are watching what you do, especially when you are a team leader.	
	Take your role seriously.	
	Take time to develop interpersonal relationships with team members, especially if team membership is permanent or long term.	
	Ask someone you trust to describe how you affect others on the team in different situations (for example, in crises or with demanding customers).	
Integrate team needs with other team, department, and organizational needs.	Map how decisions on the team will impact other functional areas. Ask others for their opinions about how the team's behaviors impact functional areas before implementing changes. Have team members explore this as a team assignment.	
	Keep track of how decisions evolve and how they affect others on the team. Have team members report on how their decisions may affect other team members.	

Continued overleaf

Table 7.1: Trust Questionnaire Formatting Example shows how you might format your questionnaire to get the most accurate and quantifiable results.

Team Trust Exercise

Here is a quick look at how you might run a meeting with your team focused on the Team Trust Audit.

Note: You can use this tool any time and multiple times with the same team. It is designed as a way of helping you "check in" with your team members and to help get and keep everyone on the same page.

TABLE 7.1 Trust Questionnaire Formatting Example

Trust Element: Keep Commitments and Show Results

1. Team members meet all deliverable cost and schedule requirements.

   ❑ Never ❑ Once in a while ❑ Sometimes ❑ Quite a bit ❑ Continually

2. In this team, we notify one another if we can't meet our commitments.

   ❑ Never ❑ Once in a while ❑ Sometimes ❑ Quite a bit ❑ Continually

3. This team does a good job of posting commitments on the network when they affect the team.

   ❑ Never ❑ Once in a while ❑ Sometimes ❑ Quite a bit ❑ Continually

4. When circumstances change, all team members hear about it in a timely manner.

   ❑ Never ❑ Once in a while ❑ Sometimes ❑ Quite a bit ❑ Continually

Instructions: The following steps constitute a one-and-one-half- to two-hour session with a team and its leader to introduce the topic of trust. However, the exercise is intended to be used in a face-to-face session whenever possible.

1. Introduce the topic of trust as an important element of leadership in the team and in the organization.

2. Ask the team members how trust promotes an effective work environment. (Responses may include facilitation of risk taking, learning, creativity, and innovation.) Also discuss the consequences of a low-trust environment.

3. Introduce the three factors of trust: performance and competence, integrity, and concern for the well-being of others. Provide some examples of each.

4. Divide the team into three subgroups. (If the session is being conducted by videoconference or audio conference, assign individuals to work on specific trust factors.) Ask each subgroup (or individual) to create a list of behaviors or actions in the team that contribute to trust.

5. Reconvene the total group and discuss the lists.

6. Distribute the Team Trust Audits and review the examples in each trust factor category. Link these items to the items presented in Step 3. Add items if appropriate.

7. Split the team into three subgroups. Assign each group (or several individuals, if the session is remote) one of the trust factor categories: performance and competence, integrity, or concern for the well-being of others. Have the subgroup members discuss the items generated in Step 4 and the items in the Team Trust Audit in relation to each of the elements in their category and decide how they could be implemented in the team.

8. Reconvene the total group and have subgroups present their results from Step 7. Discuss which items might be implemented quickly and which will be more long term. Assign time frames to actions and accountabilities.

9. Ask each person to work individually to select one item/action from each trust factor category that he or she will commit to. Ask for volunteers to discuss their actions.

10. Close the session.

11. Follow up on action items.

Keep in Touch with Other Team Members

- ❏ Check your voice mail every day and return calls within twenty-four hours.
- ❏ Check your e-mail every day and respond to messages within twenty-four hours.
- ❏ Share e-mails and documents.
- ❏ Attend all mandatory meetings.
- ❏ If you are going to be out of the office, let other people know and leave a message on your voice mail—an "out-of-the-office alert."
- ❏ E-mail messages are to be used for updating and exchanging information only. There are to be no surprises over e-mail about problems. Interpersonal issues are not to be resolved using e-mail; use the telephone or a face-to-face meeting.
- ❏ Communicate with those outside the team using our established communication plan.

Meeting Management

- ❏ Be on time for videoconferences, audio conferences, and other meetings and attend the entire meeting.
- ❏ Rotate time zones for meetings in order to be equitable and fair.
- ❏ Link times and dates to a particular time zone (for example, Eastern Standard Time in North America).
- ❏ In videoconferences or audio conferences, keep the mute button on when not speaking.
- ❏ Take breaks every sixty or ninety minutes during audio and videoconferences.
- ❏ Do not interrupt others in meetings.
- ❏ Respect the facilitator's attempts to foster participation from all team members. Respect the agenda.
- ❏ An agenda is sent out via e-mail forty-eight hours in advance of every meeting, and minutes are sent out via e-mail forty-eight hours after every meeting. Rotate taking minutes.
- ❏ If there are people attending the meeting or in the audio conference or videoconference whose native language is different from the language in which the meeting is being conducted, give them time to think and time to speak. Provide "think breaks" so that people can gather their thoughts.
- ❏ At the end of each meeting, evaluate how the team performed in terms of abiding by team norms

Continued overleaf

Decision Making and Problem Solving

❑ Strive for consensus but realize that consensus takes time and is not always necessary. If the team cannot reach consensus, go with the expert team member's opinion.

❑ Use the RSI approach to problem solving and decision making.

❑ Keep the interests and goals of the team at the forefront of all decisions.

❑ Balance the local interests of team members with those of the entire team.

❑ If you need advice, first call the team member who is considered an expert before you go outside the team.

Conflict Management

❑ Resolve differences in ways of doing business using the organization's code of conduct.

❑ Do not attempt to settle differences by using e-mail. Use the telephone and speak directly to the person. Go to the person first, not to the team leader or another team member.

❑ Use an established conflict-management process.

❑ Realize that conflict is a normal part of the team's life cycle and that conflict that is focused on the task and not on another person is healthy and productive.

❑ Recognize that unproductive conflict is more difficult to detect in a virtual setting and take the pulse of the team frequently to ensure that conflict produces positive tension. Don't let tensions build.

Working Together to Produce or Review Documents

❑ Do not review details of long documents during group audio conferences; send them to the team leader or to another designated person.

❑ When working in a sequential (assembly-line) fashion, move the document through the system in a timely manner. Give one another feedback when promised.

❑ Keep confidential documents within the core team and do not allow external team members to review them.

❑ Review the team's progress for one hour via audio conference every Monday morning. All team members are to attend, with no exceptions! All will send their agenda items and updates to the facilitator by Thursday at 5:00 P.M. (using an agreed-upon time zone, such as Eastern Standard Time in North America).

❑ The team leader is the only person who has the authority to release documents to the client.

First Day: Meeting with Your Team to Clarify Current State and Desired State

When your team is in conflict with another team, it is important that you meet with your team to discuss the problem(s). Meet with your team members and ask them these questions, taking notes:

1. Before these conflicts started, how would you define our "state" as a team?
2. Were we performing excellently?
3. What were we doing well?
4. Can you help me list specific behaviors you believe the other team is exhibiting that cause conflicts?
5. What suggestions do you have that will help us improve our coexistence with one another?
6. If the other team is receptive to our suggestions, we should be receptive to theirs. Can you do that in the spirit of cooperation?

Use the items in **Worksheet 7.2**: Sample Team Norms Checklist to discuss what your team norms are for performing effectively.

Second Day: Meeting with the Other Team's Manager to Reach Shared Understandings

Share the list of questions from the "First Day" section with the other team's manager. Meet with this person and inform him or her that you have already met as a team to discuss these questions, that you would like him or her to do the same with his or her team, and that the two of you will meet to review the findings afterward.

Before adjourning, agree to a date and time when the two of you will meet to review and share your respective findings. Look to schedule this follow-up meeting as soon as possible, preferably within one week and, also preferably, immediately after the other team's manager has had his or her team meeting.

WORKSHEET 7.3 Manager's Meeting

Goal: To help both teams improve performance

Challenges/Issues	Approaches/Solutions

Also decide with the other manager whether you believe the best approach to resolving this is manager-to-manager or team-to-team.

First Week: Facilitating Meeting of Two Managers or Two Teams to Craft Working Action Plans

Now you are proceeding with the manager-to-manager meeting or team-to-team meeting. In this manager's experience, even if you and the other manager decide to handle it yourselves, you may also benefit significantly from including at least two or three representatives from both teams.

WORKSHEET 7.4 Monthly Team Meeting

Goal: To help both teams improve performance

Challenges/Issues	Approaches/Solutions

Benefits include having exterior witnesses to the conversation, as well as getting a complete look at the teams' needs, so as to better secure desired and necessary changes that will help both teams improve performance.

Plan to make two lists, as shown in **Worksheet 7.3**: Manager's Meeting, with "Challenges/Issues" in the left-hand column and "Approaches/Solutions" in the right-hand column. The goal of this meeting is simple and straightforward: to help both teams improve their performance, in

WORKSHEET 7.5 Quarterly Team Meeting

Goal: To help both teams improve performance

Challenges/Issues	Approaches/Solutions

part by facilitating communication and cooperation between the two teams. Determine some milestones with which to measure success. Before concluding, agree to a follow-up meeting in approximately one month to review your progress.

First Month: What Has Improved? What Hasn't? Building on Success . . . or Taking Corrective Action

Now it's time to conduct your monthly team review meeting. Use **Worksheet 7.4**: Monthly Team Meeting to help you and to help team members plan action to improve performance. A tool that can help you measure progress is the Characteristics of Effective Teams, listed in this book's Introduction. Review these characteristics with each team in mind and determine how much closer you have come to the ideal level of team operations.

This tool is designed to help plan action, and to prepare you for your meeting with the other team manager.

When we find our team in conflict with another team, we need to take swift and effective action. To do so, first answer these questions:

1. Using specific behaviors, how would I describe what is happening that seems to be causing the conflict(s)?

2. What specific behaviors have we identified as "coming from the other team" that are contributing to our conflict?

3. What has anyone from the other team, especially their manager, identified as specific behaviors we are engaged in that could be contributing to our conflict?

4. When I meet with the other team's manager, what requests will I make of their team?

5. (For our meeting) What requests are they making of us?

6. (During meeting) What specific action steps have we agreed to?

Us: **Them:**

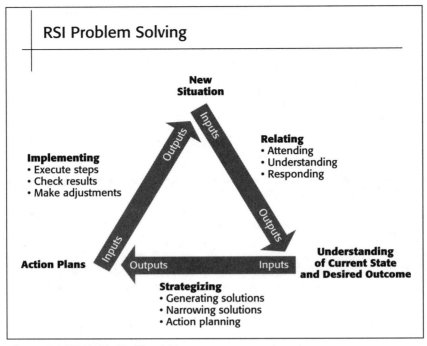

Figure 7.1 RSI Model of Problem Solving

First 90 Days: Charting Progress; Reviewing Working Relationships' Progress Against Plan

Use **Worksheet 7.5:** Quarterly Team Meeting to help you and to help team members plan action to improve performance.

Manager's Time-Out: Resolving Your Conflicts Using the RSI Model

Note: This tool is designed to help plan action and to prepare you for meeting with the other team manager.

When you are trying to resolve conflicts, you are attempting to resolve a problem. Try these thoughts on for size:

First, let's define the term *problem*. For the purpose of this discussion, we will define a problem as a situation in which there exists a gap between the current state and desired state. Let's revisit the RSI model of problem solving. *Relating* entails entering into the situation to create understanding of the existing and desired states. *Strategizing* is generating possible solutions, narrowing them to a small number based on values, and creating action plans. *Implementing* includes taking an action step, checking the result, and making necessary adjustments to the plan before continuing. As you will notice from **Figure 7.1**: RSI Model of Problem Solving, the outputs from each stage become the inputs for the next and the process becomes a continuing cycle. The purpose is not to "reinvent the wheel," but to agree on how we talk about it.

The RSI model can be used in three ways: independently, dependently, or interdependently. *Independent* application of the model occurs when you perform the steps yourself, gaining input from outside sources as needed. This is how most individual contributors work. *Dependent* application of the model is when you work with another to solve a problem, but one of you relies on the other to drive the problem-solving process. Coaching relationships, facilitated group problem solving, and mentoring are examples of dependent applications. *Interdependence* is the realm of the high-performance team. It occurs when each individual performer is competent at applying the model, and team members work together as peers to solve problems.

Let's look at the steps in the RSI model in more detail.

Relating

One of the most basic and consistent findings of research on performance is that success for individuals and teams is largely defined by their ability to create clear images of their goals. Further, the ability to generate effective strategies for attaining goals is dependent on how clearly they understand their current state.

Relating is a process for creating these images, or models. Why use the term *relating* and not the more traditional *analyzing*? Analyzing implies a separation between the observer and the phenomenon he or she observes. But detached observation is a myth. In fact, we have no choice but to relate. We can, however, relate more effectively by doing so consciously and systematically, rather than allowing our gut feelings to guide us. For example, as managers, we often look at an individual having performance problems and try to figure out what is wrong with that person. In fact, the work gets done or not done as a result of the relationship between the employee and the manager (as well as other factors). Looking at the problem from inside the *relationship* gives us a better chance of understanding why the performance isn't happening.

Strategizing

When the meaningful gap exists between the current and desired states, you continue the problem-solving process into *strategizing*. During the stages of problem solving, you continue to cycle through the relating process, constantly adjusting your images as new information becomes available.

In strategizing, you generate possible methods for achieving your goals, use your values to narrow them down to a workable few, and create action plans for each.

Implementing

The last step in the problem-solving process is *implementing*. Many plans go awry because of faulty implementation. One of the most common reasons is that performers charge through the steps without stopping to check whether the path is still leading them to their ultimate goal.

A simple method for implementing is "do-check-adjust." In essence, checking and adjusting help us continue to effectively utilize the RSI process. When you have completed a step, you *relate* to build a model of the result and compare it to the desired result. If they are the same, you go to the next step. If there is a gap, you *strategize* to create a plan for bridging the gap and adjust the plan accordingly. Finally, you *implement* the new plan and repeat the cycle. Just don't overcomplicate things.

Up next: managing and reviewing performance.

CHAPTER EIGHT

Managing Performance and Performance Reviews— Using Managing "Music" to "Soothe the Savage Breast"

Before You Start: Not Another Performance Review! Breaking Them Down over a Year into Bite-Size Gulps

The performance review process is, for many employees and managers alike, seen at best as drudgery, and at worst as torture. The employee often sees it as an ambush waiting to happen, while the manager often sees it as an unwanted, forced confrontation. As part of a larger performance management program, however, performance reviews *can be* at worst painless confirmation of feedback already given, and at best a chance to celebrate success.

When Reviewing Performance . . .

The quality of performance reviews correlates directly to the quality of performance planning. Weak performance planning results in the nonspecific goals that lead to painful performance reviews. Strong performance planning with clear goals and action plans leads to easy, painless performance reviews. Look to review performance effectively using the following steps.

Step 1: Prepare

Your Employee: Give your employee adequate lead time to prepare for a review. Fill him or her in on the process (if this is the first time). Encourage your employee by saying that you are looking forward to meeting.

The Context: Privacy in performance reviews is essential. Even strong performers are sensitive about the possibility of others overhearing them criticized. Also be conscious of seating—side-by-side seating communicates collaboration; sitting across a table or desk communicates dependency.

Yourself: If you have followed through on performance planning, you will have the performance data at hand. It is essential, when giving constructive feedback, that you have objective data to support your view of the performance. Be conscious of the approach you will take and plan the process as well as the result.

Step 2: Conduct the Meeting

Frame: Frame the meeting goals, agenda, and time.

Execute the Task: The steps in this process are the *relating* steps from the RSI model (referenced in Chapter 3 and Chapter 7)—attend, understand, respond. You can continue into *strategizing* if you wish to do performance planning directly after giving feedback, which some companies require. The actual dynamics may be independent, dependent, or interdependent. Independent processing consists of you giving feedback and getting confirmation of understanding from your employee. Processing dependently entails your leading the employee through the steps by prompting and questioning. In interdependent processing, you and the employee share observations and inferences about the performance in order to come to agreement.

Close: As always, evaluate the process, evaluate the outcomes, confirm any action steps, and incorporate the feedback into future interactions.

Step 3: Follow Up

Checking in again after an interval is especially important when engaging in performance reviews. Performers may have lingering hesitations or questions but be unable or unwilling to debrief the interaction in the moment. In addition, make sure to complete any required paperwork.

When Coaching Performance . . .

Coaching is one-on-one interaction between you and your employee for the purpose of improving performance. In a sense, it is a microcosm of performance review and performance planning. Coaching implies a perceived gap between current and desired performance and therefore calls for the RSI problem-solving process. The structure of the meeting is the same as the standard structure for personal interactions.

Step 1: Prepare

Your Employee: Inform your employee when the coaching session will be and what he or she needs to prepare. Engage the employee by asking him or her to review the specific performance before the meeting. Encourage the individual by expressing anticipation about the session.

The Context: As always, the arrangement of the meeting place will impact the interaction. Side-by-side seating encourages collaborative problem solving. You may want to have a whiteboard or flip charts available if you tend to do better explaining with pictures.

Yourself: Review previous sessions with the employee and set your goals for the session. Consciously plan an approach or agenda. Give yourself at least five minutes to relax and focus before the meeting. Refer to **Figure 8.1**: Coaching with RSI for guidance.

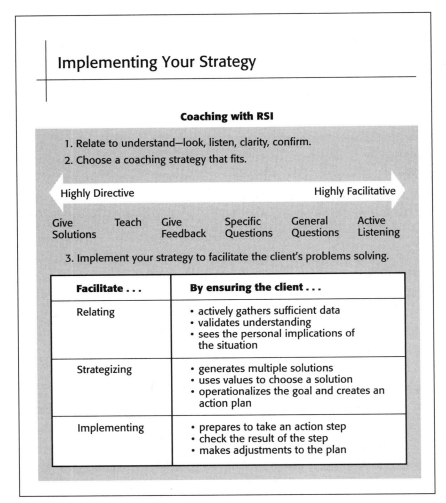

Figure 8.1 Coaching with RSI

Step 2: Conduct the Coaching Session

Frame: Frame the coaching session's time, goals, and agenda.

Execute the Task: Coaching is facilitated problem solving, so the general process will follow the RSI model. Typically you will have two objectives in coaching. The first is to enhance the employee's ability to perform his or her task. The second is to enable the employee to solve problems independently in the future. How you engage the employee depends on that person's personal style, his or her task competency, your degree of skill in the task area, and the employee's problem-solving competency.

RSI happens at two levels as you coach an employee. You, as coach, will relate to the employee to build a picture of his or her needs and your goals for the relationship. You will *strategize* to determine the best coaching approach and implement the approach as you continue to relate. You'll be helping the employee execute RSI, or some stage of the process. Your approach may vary from directive to participative, depending on the needs.

With a new employee, you may give a lot of direction initially, providing advice and instructing him or her on preferred ways of accomplishing the task. As the employee becomes more familiar with the task and the RSI process, you should be able to gradually back off until you are only acting as a sounding board and the employee drives the process. But be warned, the movement from directive to facilitative will not be smooth and linear, but full of dips and curves. It requires continuous relating on your part to choose the best approach for any given meeting.

Close: Coaching sessions should always result in a specific action plan. The results of the actions taken will become the opening of the next session. Review both the process and the results of the meeting to improve future sessions.

Step 3: Follow Up

Make sure to confirm and fulfill action agreements. Check to see how the employee is feeling after the meeting ends.

To help you in providing constructive feedback, I recommend you use **Worksheet 8.1:** Constructive Coaching Performance Checklist.

WORKSHEET 8.1 Constructive Coaching Performance Checklist

---

1. Acknowledge the Person and Actively Listen for Understanding:

    ☐ State your purpose/intentions and reservations clearly.

    ☐ Ask the person you are coaching, "How may I help you?"

    ☐ Describe the person's specific behaviors, with examples.

    ☐ Express feelings about the person's behavior.

    ☐ Make "I" or "we" statements, not judging or evaluating the person.

2. Seek, Explore, Exchange Points of View; Understand Perceptions:

    ☐ Ask for the person's perspective/position/perception.

    ☐ Listen, and pay attention to body language.

    ☐ Differentiate your and the person's positions and intentions.

    ☐ Check for accurate listening and understanding.

    ☐ Accept the person's emotions as is, without devaluing or negating them.

3. Offer Constructive Feedback, Focus on Next Steps:

    ☐ Solicit the person's preferred solution.

    ☐ Request specific behavior changes.

    ☐ Describe benefits and/or consequences of change.

4. Summarize and Close the Conversation Positively:

    ☐ Verify agreement reached and follow-up required.

    ☐ State what you have learned from the conversation.

    ☐ Express appreciation and close the conversation positively.

First Day: Reviewing Performance with Top Performer

When reviewing performance, it is important to remember that team members tend to be distributed by performance along these approximate ratios:

    5 to 15%:   Top Performers
    70 to 90%:   Average Performers
    5 to 15%:   Poor Performers

To help you ease into the performance review process, start with one of your top performers. Specifically, review with him or her:

1. What is this person doing to perform well?
2. Where could this person improve performance?
3. What steps will this person take to continue improving performance?
4. What steps will you take as manager to help this person improve performance?
5. Conclude with action plans established for both the employee and you.

Continue performance reviews in the first week, using the guidelines for reviewing average and poor performers included in the next section.

First Week: Starting to Implement Daily, One-on-One Performance Conversations with Each and Every Member of Your Team

Now, don't panic at the sound of that. Depending on how many team members you have, you most likely cannot meet with each and every team member within one week. Every member of your team is at a different place. But they all *should* hear, as soon as possible, from you:

- Their strengths
- Their areas for improvement
- Their performance improvement plan (both building on strengths and addressing areas for improvement)
- What steps you, the manager, will be taking to support their improving performance

Make sure to meet with every member of your team as soon as possible (within two weeks if not one week). Be sure to allow sufficient time for each meeting; I recommend allocating sixty minutes. If you finish sooner, focus on your other top priorities during that "found" time!

Reviewing Performance with an Average Performer

To be consistent and to reinforce especially with the vast majority who are average performers, it is important when meeting to follow this process systematically and purposefully. Again, when reviewing performance:

1. What is this person doing to perform well?
2. Where could this person improve performance?
3. What steps will this person take to continue improving performance?
4. What steps will you take as manager to help this person improve performance?
5. Conclude with action plans established for both the employee and you.

Reviewing Performance with a Poor Performer

Reviewing performance with an underperformer can be very easy or very difficult, depending on how you perceive it. I have often found this to be difficult at first, because I know (and the underperformer knows or will soon find out at the meeting) that his or her employment is at risk. Here are some tips that, in my experience, ease the tension for everyone:

1. As you prepare for the review, continue to focus on the positive.
2. As you continue to prepare, specifically for addressing shortcomings, also think about small, manageable tasks you can assign

this person so he or she can progress steadily toward improving performance.

3. As you start the review, strive to put the employee at ease. This isn't a matter of life or death; this is about improving job performance.

First Month: Met with Everyone at Least Once? Results?

Each day and then each Friday, you should allocate some time to review the outcomes of each and every one of the one-on-one meetings you had that week. In doing so, you make several gains:

1. You produce a record of the meetings that transpired (for your records).
2. By sending your summary to the person whose performance you reviewed, you give yourself and that person an opportunity to quickly, efficiently, and uniformly review his or her performance plan.
3. You give both yourself and the employee a document that can be reviewed continually and, ultimately, again when conducting that person's next performance review.

At the end of the month, review with yourself the following:

- How is each person performing against his or her plan so far?
- Are there any performance issues so serious that a quick, one-on-one meeting is warranted?
- Have I sent each team member an e-mail or a brief written report reviewing his or her performance against the plan so far, so we both can strive to be unified and consistent?

Okay, now that you've done these, you are ready to move on to the first 90 days of managing performance.

First 90 Days: Success Building, "Needs Improving" Changes, Progress Report, Next Steps

What this manager suggests you will shortly realize is that by taking a systematic approach, each day, each week, each month, and each quarter, you set yourself up for success. You also save yourself considerable time, energy, and frustration, because you have established consistent practices that become easier and easier to use over time. So, as we did in the first month, review at the end of three months:

- How is each person performing against his or her plan so far?
- Are there any performance issues so serious that a quick, one-on-one meeting is warranted?
- Have I sent each team member an e-mail or a brief written report reviewing his or her performance against the plan so far, so we both can strive to be both unified and consistent?

Assessing Team Member Competence and Performance

Here is a great opportunity to review an individual's strengths and areas for improvement. Each member of your team should fill out **Worksheet 8.2**: Assessing Team Member Competence as a competence self-assessment; meanwhile, so you can help accurately and consistently evaluate and review performance, you should do the same for each and every team member.

WORKSHEET 8.2 Assessing Team-Member Competence

Circle the level in each area of competence that best characterizes the current skills and experience of the individual being assessed (or your own skills and experience, if this is a self-assessment).

AREA OF COMPETENCE	SKILLS	SKILL LEVEL	EXPERIENCE	EXPERIENCE LEVEL
Project Management	• Can develop personal, project, and task plans, schedules, and cost estimates	1 2 3	• Has developed personal, project, or task plans, schedules, and cost estimates	1 2 3
	• Can develop different strategies to get work back on schedule		• Has shared learning in formal and informal forums	1 2 3
	• Can derive and document learnings from a number of different situations	1 2 3		
Networking	• Can identify important local stakeholders for the team	1 2 3	• Has worked in a number of different locations and functions within the organization	1 2 3
	• Can plan and implement networking activities		• Has worked with external partners, such as vendors and suppliers	
Use of Technology	• Can plan for the use of technology, given the backgrounds of team members and stakeholders and the demands of the team's task	1 2 3	• Has experience in the use of a number different communication and collaboration technologies	1 2 3

Continued overleaf

WORKSHEET 8.2 Assessing Team-Member Competence, *continued*

AREA OF COMPETENCE	SKILLS	SKILL LEVEL	EXPERIENCE	EXPERIENCE LEVEL
Use of Technology	• Can access training and skill-building activities in this area • Has worked with external partners, such as vendors and suppliers • Can plan for the use of technology, given the backgrounds of team members and stakeholders and the demands of the team's task • Can access training and skill-building activities in this area • Can plan and facilitate remote meetings	1 2 3	• Has experience in the use of a number of different communication and collaboration technologies	1 2 3

WORKSHEET 8.2 Assessing Team-Member Competence, *continued*

AREA OF COMPETENCE	SKILLS	SKILL LEVEL 1 2 3	EXPERIENCE	EXPERIENCE LEVEL 1 2 3
Self-Management	• Can plan and prioritize personal work • Can set limits and say "no" • Has personal strategies for handling ambiguity • Can identify learning opportunities		• Has worked in a number of different teams simultaneously • Has developed and executed personal-growth plans through formal education, on-the-job learning, and other strategies • Has performed tasks that required learning new skills or changes in work habits	
Crossing Boundaries	• Can constructively discuss dimensions of cultural differences • Can create ways of working that not only accommodate but optimize differences • Can plan team activities, taking into account how these processes interact with functions and cultures of team members		• Has worked in cross-functional teams • Has worked in teams with cross-organizational and/or cross-cultural representation	

WORKSHEET 8.2 *Assessing Team-Member Competence, continued*

AREA OF COMPETENCE	SKILLS	SKILL LEVEL			EXPERIENCE	EXPERIENCE LEVEL		
		1	2	3		1	2	3
Crossing Boundaries	• Can constructively discuss dimensions of cultural differences • Can create ways of working that not only accommodate but optimize differences • Can plan team activities, taking into account how these processes interact with functions and cultures of team members				• Has worked in cross-functional teams • Has worked in teams with cross-organizational and/or cross-cultural representation			
Interpersonal Awareness	• Can collect and act on feedback from others about own interpersonal style • Can give appropriate feedback, when solicited, to others regarding their styles • Can foster interpersonal interaction about styles and their impact on others				• Has worked in different situations and has modified own behavior to meet the demands of the situations • Has participated in feedback sessions on personal behaviors			

Notes: Skill level: 1 = low, 2 = medium, 3 = high

Experience level: 1 = low, 2 = medium, 3 = high

Once the worksheet is completed, total the numbers in the "Skill Level" and "Experience Level" columns. The minimum score for each column is 6 and the maximum score is 18. Interpret the numbers as follows:

Skill Level

6 to 10: You are probably just getting started in a team setting. Your challenge is to gain skill in competence areas in which you scored 1 or 2. This can be accomplished through training, reading, working with a mentor, and working in multiple teams.

11 to 14: You have a solid understanding of the requirements of team membership. Your primary challenge is to refine your skills for application in a number of different situations. This can be accomplished best by working in multiple teams under the mentorship of experienced managers.

15 to 18: You have excellent team-member skills. You may want to work on skill areas in which you scored 2 or less. You also may want to plan to help others acquire knowledge in the areas in which you are most skilled. This can be accomplished by working as a mentor/coach in multiple teams.

Experience Level

6 to 10: You probably have not had the chance to practice team membership in a corporate setting. Your challenge is to gain experience. This can be accomplished by working with a mentor or by beginning to work in teams under the guidance of experienced managers.

11 to 14: You have solid experience in a team setting. Your primary challenge is to broaden your experience in a number of different situations. This can be accomplished by working with a mentor or in multiple virtual teams.

15 to 18: You have exceptional experience in teamwork. You may want to expand your experience in any areas in which you scored 2 or less. You also may want to help others to acquire skills and experience. This can be accomplished by working as a mentor or coach in multiple teams.

Don't miss the opportunity to use a tool that is a value-added resource and will help you accurately and consistently measure, evaluate, and assess performance!

Manager's Time-Out: Managing Performance

While DISC (see Chapter 4) helps us understand individual styles, the Human Performance Equation (HPE), based on research by Dr. Raphael Vitalo, provides insight into the other factors that impact performance.

According to Dr. Vitalo, human performance is impacted by three general factors—the person performing, the information or content that person needs, and the context in which he or she performs. Each of these factors can be further broken down into subcomponents. (Breaking them down becomes useful when trying to understand why a particular task keeps failing to happen.)

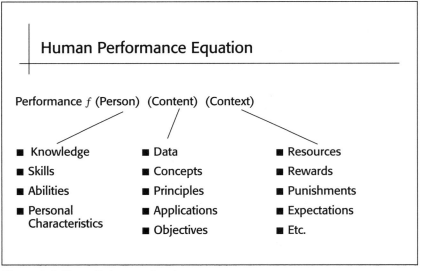

Human Performance Equation

Performance f (Person) (Content) (Context)

- Knowledge
- Skills
- Abilities
- Personal Characteristics

- Data
- Concepts
- Principles
- Applications
- Objectives

- Resources
- Rewards
- Punishments
- Expectations
- Etc.

Figure 8.2 Human Performance Equation

MANAGER'S ACTION PLAN Managing Performance–A One-Page Tip Sheet

When managing performance, keep the following in mind:

1. What is the person is doing well?

2. What could the person be doing better?

3. What action steps has the person agreed to take?

4. What action steps are you taking to support his or her improving performance?

5. At what interval (when) will you sit down together to review progress?

You're ready to take action!

Person

We naturally look to the performer first when a task is not being accomplished correctly. When doing so, it is important to understand the different aspects of a person that allow him or her to perform tasks. The aspects are generally referred to as *competencies*. Because *competency* is a word that has been overused, it is helpful to define it precisely by breaking it down into its four components—*knowledge, skills, abilities, and personal characteristics.*

Knowledge
Knowledge is the collective awareness that exists within the performer. It includes facts, concepts, principles, applications, and objectives. As a manager, for example, you need to have knowledge of HR policies and procedures.

Skills
Skills are the ability to perform a set of behaviors with some degree of competency. There are three types of skills:

- Physical Skills—e.g., juggling, typing, driving a stick shift
- Emotional Skills—e.g., dealing with anger, motivating, persuading
- Intellectual Skills—e.g., programming, project planning, writing

Abilities
Similar to skills, abilities are the capacity to perform sets of behaviors, but while skills are largely learned, abilities are more often tied to inborn traits. Some abilities may be augmented, but it usually requires a long, sustained effort to do so. There are three kinds of abilities:

- Physical Abilities—e.g., strength, endurance, hearing
- Emotional Abilities—e.g., stress tolerance, self-regulation, self motivation
- Intellectual Abilities—e.g., abstract reasoning, intuition, memory

Personal Characteristics
The dimension of personal characteristics is a catchall for attitudes, beliefs, habitual behaviors, and so on. Key to understanding personal characteristics is that they are not usually complex behaviors but simple choices. Examples include integrity, punctuality, attention to detail, loyalty, and so forth. (The DISC model is most helpful for understanding personal characteristics.)

Content

In order to accomplish a task, the performer needs specific information about the task that is sufficient for that person to complete the task to expectations. The more complex the task is, the greater the need for complete information. Content can be divided into five different types: *data, concepts, principles, applications,* and *objectives.*

Data
Data is the simplest form of information. It might include when and where the task is to be completed, for example, or a list of the tools needed. Every task requires data. For example:

- "You'll be out of town until next Tuesday."
- "The red light is blinking on the copier."
- "My idea is that we plan a team-building session."

Concepts
Concepts describe relationships among data, and are useful for specific instructions for a single task. Examples are:

- "Set your voice mail tomorrow before you leave."
- "Fix the copier."
- "Confirm what you think Mary's idea is."

Concepts allow the performance of a single task but are insufficient for more complex tasks.

Principles

Principles are rules or methods that inform the performer how to accomplish the task under a variety of conditions or circumstances, and on an ongoing basis. For example:

- "The way to program your voice mail is to [Step 1, Step 2, etc.]."
- "Follow this procedure to check the performance of the copier."
- "To check your understanding of another's idea, restate it in your own words."

You must pass on the necessary principles to the performer if he or she doesn't know how to accomplish the task already.

Applications

Applications inform the performer when and where to put the principles into use. For example:

- "Whenever you will be out of the office for more than a day, program your voice mail to automatically respond."
- "When the red light goes on, conduct the performance check on the copier."
- "Always confirm your understanding of another's idea before you criticize it."

The application level of information is needed if the performer is expected to recognize when to perform without being told.

Objectives

Objectives are the most sophisticated level of information. They indicate the larger purpose of the task. For example:

- "It's important to keep people informed of your whereabouts when you are out of town."
- "There is a big project being kept waiting because the copier is down."
- "We show our respect for people by using good communication skills."

When you want an employee to use his or her own judgment about when and how a task is performed, the employee needs to know the objective of the task. This provides the person with criteria for choosing a method.

Context

While many managers look to the person first when a task is being performed inadequately or ineffectively, more often than not the context plays a large role. This is why the RSI model (see Chapter 7) pays separate attention to context. Unlike the person and the content, context cannot be explained by a finite set of components. It can include anything in the environment that either facilitates or hinders performance. Examples of contextual factors that can strongly affect performance are:

- A manager's expectations
- Clarity of instruction
- Lack of adequate rewards
- Perceived punishments
- Lack of resources

Using the HPE

Let's look at a simple example to learn how to use the preceding concepts:
Situation: An employee shows up late to a meeting. Possible inferences:

Person
- Knowledge—He may not have known the starting time or location.
- Skills—He may lack skill in time management, which caused him to overbook his schedule.
- Abilities—He may be dealing poorly with stress, which caused him to forget the meeting.
- Personal characteristics—He may not consider punctuality important. He may like the attention he receives by being late.

Content
- Data—Employee late for meeting
- Concepts—Meeting guidelines, agenda, and participation
- Principles—Respect, professionalism
- Applications—Guidelines for effective meetings
- Objectives—Achieving goals, supporting success

Context
- He may be working on a deadline and being on time is punishing.
- The culture may reward being late as an example that one has other important things to do.
- He may be dreading something that he expects to happen in the meeting.
- He may never have received feedback that coming late is a problem.

As managers, we can only intervene to correct a performance problem if we correctly understand its cause(s). DISC and the Human Performance Equation help us as we create models of the performance. Additionally, they help us to create strategies with a high probability of success.

Now, are you ready for budgets?

CHAPTER NINE

Budgeting (Ugghh!)—Getting the Help You Need from Others to Save Yourself Time, Energy, Frustration, and Money

Before You Start: I Hate Budgets! Asking a Financial Manager for Help and Getting It

I'm going to be brutally honest with you. I hate doing budgets! Chances are, you do too.

What steps can we take to effectively understand and manage our budgets? To help ease your pain, try these simple suggestions:

1. Ask your manager for his or her perspective.
2. Ask your predecessor for his or her insights.
3. Ask a trusted colleague for his or her perspective.

If you do nothing else, meet with your manager first. During that meeting, start with these questions:

- What do you see as our top budgetary priorities? (*This is the most important question—get it answered as soon as possible.*)
- From your experience, what do you recommend we do to reduce expenses?
- What do you recommend we do to potentially increase revenues?

By next asking for your predecessor's perspective, if that is at all possible, you will receive some experience-based insights for managing your own budget. Your predecessor's recommendations can only enhance your perspective and support your action steps.

Here is one of several opportunities I will take to suggest initiating and cultivating manager-peer working relationships. By asking a managerial colleague for his or her perspective and recommendations pertaining to your budget, you are both letting your colleague know you value his or her opinion and providing that person with an opportunity to ask for your help, if needed. From my experience, taking this approach in any arena—and *especially* in dealing with that "employee who just drives me crazy"—is a great way to develop good, productive working relationships, which will serve you well not just for the rest of your working life, but for the rest of your life, period!

On to implementing the budget. . . .

First Day: Meeting with Manager-Helper; Presenting Data; Receiving Brutally Honest Feedback; Action Planning

Let's remember that a budget, as defined by the dictionary, is:

- An itemized summary of estimated or intended expenditures for a given period along with proposals for financing them
- A systematic plan for the expenditure of a usually fixed resource, such as money or time, during a given period
- The total sum of money allocated for a particular purpose or period of time

All three of these definitions speak to the critical time-sensitivity of budgets, so it is very important to take what your manager has told you are your top budgetary priorities and start implementing them. Remember, if you get no other question answered, get this one answered: "What do you see as our top budgetary priorities?" Start implementing your manager's answer *today*.

First Week: Budget Action Planning, Progress Against the Top Three Priorities

When you engage in your first team meeting, be sure to do the following:

- Include the budget as an agenda item.
- Share with the entire team what your manager has told you (as long as you are not breaching any confidentialities).
- Let the team know what steps you are planning to take to address these budgetary priorities.
- Ask team members what they believe they can do to support the team's budgetary priorities (if they don't come up with suggestions on their own, ask some leading questions to get them engaged).
- Respond to any questions team members may have.
- Clarify and confirm the team's action steps.

Be sure to involve each and every member of your team to the greatest extent possible in understanding and helping you to manage your budget. When I worked for Marriott, they involved employees (and I believe they still do) in supporting safety and in profit sharing. This was extraordinarily productive, and helped us cut costs related to safety, which in turn enhanced our profit sharing. It's a great example of how everyone benefits from involving team members in the enterprise.

First Month: Budgeting Monthly, Progress Reporting

Make sure you and your manager are in agreement on the annual budget, as well as monthly and quarterly targets. Plot out your monthly and quarterly targets, and start supporting your team's efforts to reach those targets on a daily and weekly basis. That's right; by breaking down these bigger targets into smaller units (daily and weekly), you make them more manageable and achievable!

Post whatever information you can; this keeps people involved and informed.

Make these three questions part of the team and workplace daily conversations:

1. What steps are we taking to achieve our monthly goals? (Start with the bigger target, so people get a better sense of the "bigger picture.")
2. What steps are we taking to achieve our daily goals?
3. What steps are we taking to achieve our weekly goals?

Make sure you keep yourself, your manager, and your team informed with monthly, biweekly, and/or weekly reports. Place these three questions at the top of any communication regarding budgets—or any other aspect of your enterprise that gets people thinking, speaking, and *taking action*!

First 90 Days: Budgeting Quarterly, Verifying Progress

Keep the budget momentum going! Continue using your three questions and facilitating your "budget conversations" with your manager—and especially your team members—as frequently as possible.

Need we say more? Go for it!

Remember, your manager's priorities are your priorities, especially when it comes to budgeting. Answer these questions:

1. What does my manager tell me my top budgeting priorities are?

2. What steps am I taking to implement these priorities?

3. By when (deadlines) are these priorities to be implemented? (Be sure to schedule in your Outlook or scheduling software.)

4. When am I informing my team of our budgetary priorities?

You're good to go!

Manager's Time-Out: Budgeting

As some people have said over the years, "Don't worry; it's only money!"

Seriously, let's keep everything in its proper perspective: human life and health come before anything and everything else. If you have any life and/or health issues to deal with, be it yourself or a member of your family, be sure to mention it to your boss as well as someone in Human Resources or your Employee Assistance Program; that is a big part of the reason they are there.

Now that you have started prioritizing your budget and budgeting, think about this. According to the American Management Association, the "Essentials of Budgeting" include the following:

Key Objectives
- Define a budget.
- Distinguish among the different types of budgets.
- Discuss and evaluate budget variances.
- Explain the impact of external factors to budgeting, forecasting, and strategy.
- Use tools to prepare and justify your budget.

Budget Fundamentals
- Explain what a budget is and why organizations create them.
- Identify the components of a budget.
- Identify who within an organization should be involved in the development of a budget.
- Explain where creating a budget fits into the corporate planning/budgeting cycle.
- Discuss how a company's budget influences its financial statements.

Develop a Budget
- Define various types of budgets.
- Explain the advantages/disadvantages of each type of budget.
- Develop a budget.

Measure Performance Against the Plan
- Discuss why variance analysis is important.
- Compare and contrast recent past performance versus budget.
- Determine how to address and control variances.

Capital Budgets
- Define a capital budget and its components.
- Define why capital budgets are vital to an organization.
- Calculate capital budgeting ratios.
- Define factors for capital budget approvals.
- Explain how capital budgets affect the P&L and balance sheets.

The Impact of External Factors
- Identify external factors.
- Define *forecasting.*
- Define *strategy.*
- Recognize the relationship of external factors to budgeting, forecasting, and strategy.
- Recommend ways to minimize the impact of external factors.

Prepare and Justify Your Budget
- List the dos and don'ts of preparing your budget.
- List the dos and don'ts of justifying your budget.
- Demonstrate justifying your budget.

Hopefully, these highlights give us a context for learning more about budgets and budgeting. If you would like more information, the American Management Association manages a very popular instructional budgeting workshop program.

Look them up at www.amanet.org.

From Forming to Performing—
The Top Ten Ways to Develop a
Managing "Rhythm" That
Works for You and Your Team

Before You Start: In Which "Stage" Is Our Team?

Over the last fifty years, quite a few researchers and other experts in group dynamics have sought to describe and explain how teams develop and mature. The seminal work in this area was a 1965 research paper by Bruce Tuckman of the Naval Medical Research Institute at Bethesda (Tuckman, "Forming, Storming, Norming, and Performing in Groups," 1965). In the years that followed, various authors have suggested models ranging from two to seven or more stages, and using a variety of different names for the stages. But most have centered on the four basic stages hypothesized by Tuckman. The four stages we will describe here are based on Tuckman's original work.

Tuckman recognized that, in talking about how small groups develop, you have to consider two aspects of the four stages: the interpersonal (group structure) and the task behaviors. As we discuss each of the four stages, remember that these two aspects are very different, yet so closely integrated that you can't address one without the other.

During the first stage, *forming*, teams are testing out group norms and trying to define the boundaries of their task.

In the second, or *storming*, stage, there is friction and jockeying for position among members, which may produce emotional responses. (Tuckman found, however, that extreme emotion about the task itself is rare if the tasking deals with impersonal work issues.)

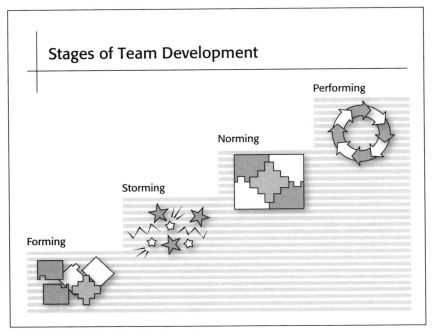

Figure 10.1 Stages of Team Development

The third stage, *norming*, represents a time of change in which interdependence develops within the group and members become more willing and able to express opinions and ideas constructively.

In the final stage, *performing*, group members begin to apply their "oneness" to the task at hand, developing solutions and making progress.

Now that you have a brief picture of the four stages, let's take a closer look at each one, and see what you can do as the manager to help the team progress from one stage to the next.

Stage 1: Forming

Forming is the word used to describe the first stage of the team's development. In this stage, the group is first coming together with the goal of becoming a team. Team members' behaviors, prompted by their feelings of excitement, anxiety, and dependence, raise certain issues, which must be resolved if the team is to mature.

Members may feel:

- *Excited.* They may be eager to participate and look forward to a new undertaking.
- *Anxious.* They may feel some anxiety about what the team will accomplish, about working in a team setting, or about working with people they don't know.
- *Dependent.* They may feel uneasy about relying on others for success or unsure about what they can contribute.

These feelings may bring up the following issues:

- *Testing authority.* How do members balance the desire to test authority figures with their dependence on these same figures to help the team get started?
- *Inclusion.* How do members feel about fitting in and meeting other team members' expectations?
- *Trust.* How does the team get members to feel comfortable and develop trust in their fellow team members, their team leader, and the process?

Because of all of the turmoil at the group process level, teams in this stage usually do not make much progress on their charter assignment. The team must address these issues openly and honestly. If there are significant problems, these need to be resolved. During this stage, the team manager's guidance is tested and it's up to the manager to channel the team's energy productively.

Leaders can help by:

- *Adding structure.* It is important during the forming stage to hold structured meetings, which help to focus discussions, clarify tasking, and define roles.
- *Encouraging learning.* Members need to ask each other questions to find out about expertise within the group and differences or similarities in how each individual works. It may be helpful to put this information in the context of defined personality types, such as the Keirsey-Bates or Myers-Briggs categories.
- *Balancing participation.* Balanced participation is an important aspect of effective teamwork. A team leader should set the pace for balancing participation by encouraging everyone to participate and by discouraging dominant behavior, especially in the first few meetings.

Stage 2: Storming

Now let's look at Stage 2 of the team's development, called *storming*. Team members begin to realize the amount of work that lies ahead and start to panic. They may flail about like people who think they are drowning.

During this stage, members realize the task is more complicated than anticipated. They see a disparity between the hopes they felt for the team when it first formed and the reality of the work ahead of them. The aptness of the weather analogy implicit in the term storming will become apparent as we describe the characteristics of this stage.

Members may feel:

- *Incompetent and confused.* They may not be sure they have the skills to do their task. They may be confused about how to proceed.
- *Frustrated.* They may feel frustrated by the requirements of the team situation, the time it takes to get thing done, and other factors.

- *Negative.* They may have negative feelings about the leader and other team members.

These feelings may bring up the following issues:

- *Power.* Who can make it happen?
- *Control.* Who will be in charge?
- *Conflict.* How do team members resolve conflicts based on differences of opinion?

The destructive behaviors often seen in the storming stage can seem unpleasant and unnecessary. However, much of it may be unavoidable since storming is a part of the natural evolution of teams. We will learn more later about how to manage conflict effectively, sometimes even making it productive. For now, recognize that there are a few basic things team leaders and quality advisors can do to help teams through this stage of development.

Leaders can help by:

- *Facilitating dialogue.* As differences of opinion emerge, the team leader should encourage members to constructively state their ideas and feelings. Only by expressing what they think and feel can the group begin to understand each other's views and effectively resolve their conflicts.
- *Helping with decision making.* Groups in the storming stage need guidance in identifying how they will make decisions and solve problems. The quality advisor or team leader should help them explore alternatives and decide what will work best, then help them through the content of some decisions that will move the team forward in their tasking.
- *Providing support.* The team is very vulnerable at this point because of the airing of emotions and differing points of view. To be effective, leaders must closely monitor group process and content issues that could derail the team. Support such as providing

resources, reaffirming their purpose and capabilities, and running interference with outside groups is especially important now.

Stage 3: Norming

During Stage 3, referred to as *norming*, members get used to working together. They start helping each other rather than competing. They have resolved some of the conflict they felt in Stage 2 and begin acting more like a team.

Members may feel:

- *Open to constructive feedback.* They are more comfortable with both giving and receiving feedback.
- *Accepted by the team.* Team members feel accepted by the team and begin to work together more effectively.
- *Comfortable.* Their anxieties about the task may start to subside.

These feelings may bring up the following issues:

- *Team harmony.* How does the team develop trust, respect, and support on the part of all team members?
- *Shared responsibility.* How can team members learn to work together?
- *Building confidence.* How can the team develop full confidence in its ability to perform?

During the norming stage, the task of the team leader or quality advisor is to help the team adjust to its newfound identity and self-confidence. Leaders can help by:

- *Backing off.* As the team becomes more independent, it is time for the leader to begin delegating more responsibility to team members, encouraging them to run more of the meetings themselves and to make decisions on their own. This is difficult for some people to do, so it is important to make a conscious effort to let go.

- *Expressing own ideas.* As groups become more self-assured, they are better able to hear others' issues and concerns. If the team leader has been holding off on stating personally held thoughts about content or group process, this is the time to express them. This may provide the fresh perspective needed to keep the team out of the "groupthink" mode.
- *Challenging them.* "Norming" teams may need more challenging assignments to continuously improve their skills. Asking them to, for example, independently reach consensus on a high-stakes issue can be an important growth opportunity.

Stage 4: Performing

The final stage is the *performing* stage. Team members have become comfortable with each other and their project. They are an effective working unit with everybody "singing from the same sheet of music." The concern of the team is success. At this stage, the team really begins to perform competently.

Members may feel:

- *Appreciative of each other's strengths.* Work performance is high as team members build on each other's strengths.
- *Accepting of each other's weaknesses.* Team members help each other accomplish their goal and support the efforts of all members.
- *Satisfied with their progress on the task.* Team members feel positive about their successes.
- *Confident in their abilities as a team.* The team is now an effective, cohesive unit—a "winning team."

- *Optimistic.* The team is confident that they can accomplish tasks.

These feelings may bring up the following issues:

- *Goal accomplishment.* The team may have some questions about their ability to achieve team goals and milestones.
- *Maintaining momentum.* The team may be unclear how to continue building, once they have achieved certain milestones.

The primary task of the leader for teams in the performing stage is to help members develop group maintenance skills.

Leaders can help by:

- *Suggesting new goals.* As team members approach completion of the original task with self-confidence, they need to start thinking about what lies ahead. They may require some gentle guidance to help them decide about future goals and opportunities.
- *Testing assumptions.* Team members in the performing stage typically develop such comfort in their ways of behaving and working together that they risk becoming complacent about their ability to function well as a team. This is a good time to question their assumptions about group norms or ground rules, and challenge members to determine if new or additional ones might be needed.
- *Developing self-assessment processes.* To become truly self-sufficient, a team must have in place a specific mechanism for ongoing self-assessment. The leader should suggest procedures, timing, and format for members to evaluate both their individual performance and how they function together as a team.

Understanding these stages of growth will help you react effectively to the changing behaviors of the team. Be patient. It may take as long as four to six months to get a team performing well together.

Many factors can affect a team's progress: the size of the group, the mix of personalities, the frequency of meetings, the level and visibility of the task, and the experience level of the leader. The main thing to keep in mind is that virtually all teams eventually arrive at the performing stage.

Cycling Through the Stages

Unfortunately, teams don't stay in the performing stage indefinitely. Significant changes in team membership such as the replacement of a leader, a change in the team purpose, or changes in team processes will throw the team back into the forming stage. Your job is to help the team cycle back through the stages to performing as *effectively* as possible. Notice the use of effectively rather than *quickly*. Trying to force the team back through the stages too quickly can cause the team to become stuck.

If nothing else, before you meet with your team, ponder this: as either a new manager or a manager taking a fresh approach to your team, you are in the forming or "re-forming" stage—Stage 1.

First Day: Meet with Team to Share Assessment; Ask for Solution Input; Action Planning

It is important that you keep team members informed. One thing that might help you get everyone on board to support the team's success is to share with them an article about teams (shoot me an e-mail at cdevany@ppiw.com or via our Web site at www.ppiw.com, and I'll be glad to send you one), as well as telling them the following:

> Right now, because I am new as your manager [or taking a fresh approach to this team], we are in the forming or "re-forming" stage, so this is my understanding:

1. I have done my best to convey our goals, which are [state goals]. Any questions? Do we all know what action steps we are taking from this point forward?

2. We are encouraging learning by agreeing that all questions are helpful and a sign of interest. Asking questions is how we all learn, so let's keep asking questions, which will help each and all of us to continue improving performance as a team.

3. I am doing my best to support your participating in our team's success. Please let me know at any time what I can do to support your success, knowing that I will, after responding to your request, also ask you what steps you are taking to support your success.

4. So, what do we understand are our Top Three Team Goals?

Be sure to post your Top Three Team Goals somewhere so everyone can see them every day. This is your team's "Top Three Mantra."

First Week: Progress Against Action Plan?

Some will suggest that one week is too short a time period to measure success; I will go absolutely and firmly against that "conventional wisdom" by stating that, if we are not measuring our success daily and weekly, then how can we expect to realize any longer-term success?

So, with this in mind, ask people:

- "How are we doing against our daily and weekly goals?"
- "What (if any) short-term corrective action do we need to take?"
- "How are we doing so far against our Top Three Team Goals?"

First Month: Have We "Hit" Our Top Three Goals? What Are the Characteristics of Effective Teams?

As you are asking your team members, "How are we doing against our monthly team goals?" and "How did we do against our first month's goals?" be sure to also ask:

- "What are we doing well?"
- "What steps can we take to keep building on our strengths?"
- "What could we be doing better?"
- "What steps can we take to improve on what we could be doing better?"

For you and your team to succeed, you need to understand both:

- How to build on your strengths
- What steps to take to address improvement

If each and every one of us spent at least as much time understanding what we do well and building on our strengths as we do beating ourselves up over our weaknesses, we'd all be much better off as human beings.

According to research by Carl Larson and Frank LaFasto, (Larson and LaFasto, *When Teams Work Best*, 2001) effective teams share eight characteristics:

1. *A Clear and Elevating Goal*
   Effective teams have goals that are unambiguous and easy to understand. They are also goals that inspire team members to perform at their best.
2. *A Results-Driven Structure*
   Effective teams are organized in ways that take advantage of individual strengths and enable collective effort.

3. *Competent Team Members*
   Effective teams have members who have strong technical and interpersonal skills.

4. *Unified Commitment*
   Effective teams have members who are aligned with their goals and place achievement of goals above personal success.

5. *Collaborative Climate*
   Effective teams have an internal culture that supports honest, open communication.

6. *Standards of Excellence.*
   Effective teams settle for nothing less than the best results. They win by outperforming their competitors.

7. *External Support and Recognition*
   Effective teams have the resources they need and the support of the organization in which they exist. They receive consistent rewards for the excellence they produce.

8. *Principled Leadership*
   Effective teams have leaders that are values-based. They keep the team focused on the task while enabling growth of team members.

As a manager, you are responsible for the performance of your team. Knowing the characteristics of effective teams allows you to pinpoint your team's strengths and areas for improvement. These characteristics also become tools for relating and strategizing with your team. They help you to model your team's current situation by giving you dimensions and help you to strategize by expanding your range of solutions.

First 90 Days: After Three Months, What Do We Do to Continue Growing? Team Member and Team Action Plans

In supporting success and then measuring progress against quarterly goals, a quick reminder about those important questions:

- "How did we do against our quarterly goals?"
  —"What are we doing well?"
  —"What steps can we take to keep building on our strengths?"
  —"What could we be doing better?"
  —"What steps can we take to improve in those areas?"
  —"What steps can we take daily to support our success?"

Before we conclude, let's take a look at our Manager's Action Plan and Manager's Time-Out for this chapter . . .

Troubleshooting, and Keeping Your Team on Track

There will be times when you'll need to reevaluate your team's progress, or help team members change direction when they've veered off course. Here are a few tools to help with that.

You can use **Worksheet 10.1:** A Collaboration Progress Checklist anytime, just to take the temperature of your team and see what sort of progress you're making toward your goals.

Table 10.1: Team Process Interventions Checklist can be used to diagnose and address larger problems within the team. These may cause the sorts of problems discussed in the previous chapters, but need attention on a deeper, more systemic level. Look at the various categories of problems and see which one best describes your team.

WORKSHEET 10.1 A Collaboration Progress Checklist

Factors	Strongly Agree 1	Somewhat Agree 2	Neither Agree Or Disagree 3	Somewhat Disagree 4	Strongly Disagree 5
Goals					
Communication					
Sustainability					
Research/Evaluation					
Political Climate					
Resources					
Catalysts					
Policies/Laws/Regulations					
History					
Connectedness					
Leadership					
Community Deveopment					
Understanding Community					
Total					
Grand Total					

TABLE 10.1 Team Process Interventions Checklist

Symptom of Team Problem	Possible Interventions by the Team Leader
The team cannot get out of the inception and inclusion stage. (Possible questioning of purpose)	Teams that get stuck in the first stage have larger underlying issues. Review the team's composition and the team's charter. Ensure that the right people are on the team and that they understand the charter. The inception phase requires creativity and less control. Be sure that you are modeling creativity and not overcontrolling the members. If possible, bring in a member from the organization who is innovative to challenge and spark the team.
The team appears to be stuck and is not moving toward execution. (Possible questioning of accountabilities).	Assess the team in terms of task and social dynamics. Discuss the problem with the team. Look at environmental factors that may be causing the team to slow down. Also look at the team's work practices and determine if the members need help in establishing priorities or a reasonable work schedule. Hold a session to review expectations. Map the team's progress and problems to see if any patterns appear that need to be changed in order to allow the team to move forward.
A few team members seem to be doing all the work. (Possible questioning of accountabilities, norms, protocols, and/or maximizing team participation).	Talk to the working and nonworking members separately to determine the reasons for the differences. Are tasks allocated appropriately? Are the working members creating an exclusive environment, because of national or functional cultures, that is keeping the others out? Do the nonworkers feel that there is something wrong with the team or its leadership?
Team members do not appear to be applying sufficient effort to the team's task. (Possible questioning of accountabilities and/or maximizing team participation).	Address this problem quickly. First, talk to the team members who are not applying the required effort and determine whether the problem lies with them or with another factor, such as unrealistic expectations. If the problem is the individuals, find out why they are not putting forth the effort. If the problem stems from lack of skills or resources, get them the training or resources they need. If it stems from

TABLE 10.1 Team Process Interventions Checklist, *continued*

Symptom of Team Problem	Possible Interventions by the Team Leader
	attitudes, talk to them about it. Do they feel the work is meaningful? Are they receiving timely feedback on their work? Are the results of their work recognized?
The team misses or almost misses a deadline for deliverables. (Possible questioning of focus on team outcomes and results and/or maximizing team participation).	If the team is likely to miss a deadline, find out the reason. Put the mechanisms in place to fix the problem. Communicate to your executive sponsor that you have corrected the problem. During the next cycle, stay close to the team. It is better to be accused of micromanaging than to miss a deadline for a deliverable. Talk with and monitor the team members. When their progress becomes satisfactory, you can pull back.
Conflict arises that derails the team's progress. (Possible questioning of focus on team outcomes and results).	Discover the reason for the conflict. If it is task related, review the work plan and seek input on how to improve the problem. If it is social in nature, determine the cause and determine if differences in culture are indicated. If it is between two individuals, speak with both of them individually. If the conflict involves you, ask an outside facilitator to help to resolve the problem.
Team members who are not colocated seem to be fading into obscurity. (Possible questioning of accountabilities, maximizing team participation, and/or communication).	Virtual team members can fall into obscurity. Keep a record of when you have contact with members. Set up a schedule and be sure to talk with or meet with each team member regularly through e-mail, telephone calls, visits, and so forth. Sometimes go to where the members are; don't always ask them to come to you. If some members are not in the team on a full-time basis, their other priorities may be taking them away from the team. Talk to their supervisors and review the agreements that you made before they were assigned to your team. Sometimes it is necessary to ask team members who are located together to meet informally to keep up morale.

What is critical to keep in mind about helping your team to achieve maximum performance are the following:

1. You need to inform everyone of your team goals.

2. You need to remind your team of your organization goals.

3. You need to remind everyone of your customers' goals.

4. You should facilitate individual team members at a team meeting speaking to their personal performance (team member) goals.

5. You should give team members a chance to tell you privately if they are not comfortable speaking up publicly.

6. You should post, in one place, next to each other, the following:

Team Goals:	Organization Goals:	Customer Goals:	Team Member Goals:

By posting these side by side, you give everyone on your team a chance to see how what they do helps you, as a team and as an organization, achieve your goals, as well as helping your customers achieve their goals in doing business with your company!

Manager's Time Out: Team Building

This is a brief reflection; answer for yourself the following:

1. What do I like about the work I do?
2. What do I like about the people I work with?
3. When was the last time I told my team members my answers to these two questions and then asked them the same two questions?

Next, get ready to explore managing others at multiple locations and from a distance.

PART TWO

ADDITIONAL TOOLS AND RESOURCES

CHAPTER ELEVEN

So Far Away—
Managing Remote and Virtual Teams

O NE OF THE BIGGEST CHALLENGES for managers today is teams wherein some or all members are stationed in remote locations. Many corporations are working to reduce the significant costs of travel usually associated with teams of people located in several countries. Colleagues may not interact frequently; some may not even know each other. Increasingly, global teams are required to learn to work effectively in the absence of regular face-to-face interactions, which presents a variety of problems.

So, the occasional glitch will be inevitable, but there are many things you can do to make virtual team functioning as painless as possible. The first step is to make sure everyone understands and respects the situation. **Table 11.1:** Four-Step Process to Gain Agreement on Team Outcomes lists some items you'll want to communicate to your team:

This is best done during your first "in-person" meeting as a team.

Meeting "in person" is important for all newly formed teams, regardless of cultural preferences. It is especially important to those team members with a cultural preference for relationship—those who prefer to get to know someone before trust can be built (as in many Asian business cultures).

By the end of this chapter, you will be able to:

1. Boost productivity at every location.
2. Significantly cut down on paperwork.
3. Know off-site employees are following rules and implementing proper policies and procedures.
4. Spot problems even when you're far away.
5. Choose appropriate technology for remote teams.
6. Effectively use various technologies.

Before Starting and the First Day: Communication and Problem Solving

Communication is about working with others to solve problems.

We define a problem as any situation in which there is a gap between our current state and our desired state. This doesn't imply that our current state is wrong or bad, but simply that there is some other state in which we would rather be.

Problem solving begins by *relating* to the world around us. We *attend*, or pay attention, to what is going on around us. This gives us observations, or data. We try to *understand* this data using our existing knowledge and beliefs. We then *respond* to the current state by asking ourselves, "Is there a meaningful gap between this state and the state in which I'd like to be?" If the answer is yes, we have at least an implied desired outcome.

When we've identified a meaningful gap, we create *strategies* for bridging it by *generating* solutions that we might use, *narrowing* these solutions to those that we like best, and converting the solutions to action plans.

Once we have an action plan, we begin to *implement* it by executing a step in our plan, *check the results* against our plan, and *make adjustments* to the plan as necessary. Each step creates a new situation and causes the problem-solving process to start anew until there is no longer a meaningful gap between our current and desired states.

In order to apply the RSI problem-solving model to working with others, we need some knowledge about how people perceive the world and act based on their perceptions.

Week One: Giving People a Road Map for Problem Solving and Team Building

To give your location managers and team members a business road map that will keep them headed in the right direction, we suggest an eight-step process to help you.

TABLE 11.1 Four-Step Process to Gain Agreement on Team Outcomes

Communicating	Establishing Expectations	Allocating Resources	Modeling Behaviors
• Communicate the business necessity of virtual teams.	• Define how virtual teams work and set clear procedures and goals.	• Allocate time and money for training for virtual team leaders and members.	• Align cross-functional and regional goals and objectives.
• Communicate that virtual teamwork is respected.	• Set high standards for virtual team performance.	• Allocate time and money for travel for team leaders for face-to-face meetings.	• Work together on management team performance across geographic and cultural boundaries.
• Discuss the value of diversity and of leveraging skills.	• Establish expectations of customers and other important stakeholders.		• Solicit input from and display trust in team members.
• Communicate the benefits and results of working virtually.	• Factor in start-up costs and times.		• Show flexibility.

Step One: Organize a Team Meeting

Where should you start? Practical steps for preparing include:

- Plan your meeting as far in advance as possible, at least two weeks ahead, including meeting objectives and an agenda. Reinforce the importance and benefits of attending.
- Prepare a background and introduction, communicating what you want to say to your team. Include why you are here and what you hope to accomplish.
- Be prepared to lead, guide, and share vision. Describe what success would look like for your team, both short term and long term.
- Be prepared to articulate your team's mission and how it supports your company's mission, vision, and values.

Step Two: Prepare an Agenda

Some suggestions for what to include on the agenda:

- Team mission
- Your vision
- Team goals
- Individual introductions
- Listing of scheduled team projects, in conjunction with team goals
- Assigning roles to individuals
- Soliciting comments and feedback as the meeting progresses. This will help each team member answer the question, "What role do I play in this process?"

Step Three: Facilitate the Agenda

To help you manage your meetings even more effectively, consider the following process (Ten-Step Meeting Process):

1. Assure that everyone has a copy of the meeting agenda in advance.
2. Appoint a timekeeper.
3. Choose a person to take minutes.
4. Approve the last meeting's minutes.
5. Proceed with the agenda.
6. Defer non-agenda items to the Parking Lot.
7. Stick to the time schedule, unless a majority votes otherwise.
8. Delegate action items/ensure individual responsibility.
9. Assess the meeting process, schedule the next meeting, and adjourn.
10. Distribute meeting minutes to meeting attendees within forty-eight hours.

Step Four: Distribute and Discuss a Communication Plan

For a communication plan to work, people need to know:

- *Who:* Who is on our team? Who (if any) are our external stakeholders?
- *What:* What are the tasks and projects we will be addressing as a team? To whom are they assigned?
- *When:* By when do we need to accomplish each of our tasks?
- *How:* How will we communicate with each other? Which communication methods will we use?

Step Five: Discuss and Clarify Norms and Protocols

- What will our team norms and protocols be? For example, how frequently will you be meeting with your location managers? How frequently will your location managers be meeting with their team members?

*Step Six: Establish a Ground Rule: Everyone Is Accountable,
            Including You*

- The best way to encourage and facilitate team participation is
  to model the behavior you expect from others. Be accountable
  first, so others may follow.

Step Seven: Identify Action Items for Everyone

- What is/are each person's action item(s)?
- Every location manager and team member should have at least
  one action item; be sure everyone does.

Step Eight: Distribute Meeting Minutes Within Forty-Eight Hours

- The sooner meeting minutes are distributed, the sooner everyone is
  on the same page.

First Month: Procedures, Policies, and Actions That Will Help Your "Extended Team" Come Together

Procedures

You need to have some procedures in place to make things work well. You
want these procedures to be crystal clear. Some suggestions for creating
crystal-clear procedures that off-site staff will follow to the letter include
a four-step process:

1. *Outline specific procedures*—Read what is written privately to
   yourself before distributing. Do you understand clearly what is
   meant? If not, review and rewrite.

2. *Provide steps*—Giving your team a clear, linear set of steps to follow will save everyone time, energy, and frustration.

3. *Include/clarify reporting process*—With what frequency and which communication method will you use in the reporting process? For example, if there is a weekly report to be submitted, by what time on what day of the week is it to be submitted? Do you want it e-mailed or hard copied?

4. *Regularly check to clarify and confirm (verify)*—Provide your contact information if anyone has any questions. Allocate time in team meetings for same.

Policies

You want to be able to quickly smooth things over when you have to lay down the law and enforce an unpopular policy . . . from a distance. There are four steps we can follow to help us with this challenge:

1. Schedule the agenda item on the next group conference call: "Discuss _____ policy."

2. Prepare for discussion by understanding and writing down the rationale for the policy.

3. Anticipate challenges to the policy by listing them and your responses (rehearsal). Remind everyone of the value to the team for enforcing the policy.

Actions

The actions you must take if you want to slow down the "paper blizzard" include:

1. Verify your team communication plan and norms and protocols.
2. Ensure there are standard reporting forms distributed and available electronically.
3. Communicate clearly how frequently certain forms are to be submitted.
4. If a location manager needs to communicate with you about a personnel matter, establish the following guidelines for location managers. They should:

   a. Compose an e-mail describing the situation.
   b. Include in the e-mail message how they tried to solve it or how they wish to solve it.
   c. Contact you by e-mail, requesting a date and time for discussion.
   d. As they are composing the message, they should ask themselves, "Am I already empowered to solve this?" If so, they should try to solve it and save both of you some time.

Keeping Your Finger on the Pulse

You want to keep your finger on the pulse of off-site action without making employees feel like Big Brother is watching.

We all understand that communication is essential to support team and company success, just as we appreciate the reality that we can't be everywhere at all times.

The best way to stay on top of things is to engage your location managers in weekly communication of some sort, either a conference call or e-mail. This way, you ensure that at least once a week, you and your location managers are "on message." Also, this weekly staying in touch reminds location managers to contact you if they need your help.

Note: Whenever you facilitate a team meeting or conference call, be sure a written record of the meeting or call ("meeting minutes") is distributed within forty-eight hours. This will keep everyone on the team together.

Responsibilities That Are Yours and Yours Alone

To manage effectively, you want to know what responsibilities you must shoulder alone . . . and when you can safely share the load with location managers and employees.

To save time, energy, and frustration, you want to empower your location managers to make decisions and manage more effectively. You will best empower your managers by modeling the behavior you expect from them and by letting them know that you will support their efforts any way possible.

It is essential that you must manage and be solely responsible for supporting and monitoring location manager performance.

You must also:

- *Plan*—Plan for performance or be prepared to fail.
- *Organize*—Keep an orderly work space.
- *Communicate*—Regularly inform your location managers what you expect of them and what you expect of yourself.
- *Monitor*—Check in with each location manager, both during team meetings and individually.
- *Delegate*—Empower your location managers, just as you want them to empower their employees.

Share this approach with each of your location managers; have them adopt the same process and approach in order to ensure consistency and collaborative support.

Quality Control

To quickly and accurately check the quality of products or services at any location, we can think of at least three effective methods, including:

1. *Mystery Shopper*—Someone you authorize anonymously arrives and poses as a potential customer, to verify performance.
2. *Surprise Visit*—You arrive unannounced.
3. *Customer Satisfaction Reports*

Inside Secrets

The inside secrets to creating a lasting bond between location managers so everyone feels as if they're on the same team start with building a team mentality and team spirit. These are critical to gaining your location managers' support, participation, and commitment to improving performance. We encourage you to consider and practice the following:

1. Constantly look for ways to recognize successful performers.
2. Ask each location manager to recognize one of their peers.
3. Let everyone know, and *you facilitate*, team discussion where any location manager can bring a problem or issue to the team for help.
4. Support "peer pairs"—peer helping peer.
5. Practice constructive feedback principle of "two pieces of praise for each piece of criticism"—we learned this from Toastmasters.
6. Whenever discussing individual performance, always couch the behavior and results as to "How does this impact our team?"
7. Support and facilitate team-building activities—including group process, pizza parties, bowling, or other activities . . . you get the idea.

First 90 Days: Gaining Consensus and Building a "Winning" Team Structure—The Ten Principles That Will Help You Today, Tomorrow, and Beyond

Gaining Consensus

To build the support you need and to facilitate your location managers' independence, one of your most effective tools is gaining and building consensus.

What's the best way to conduct consensus decision making? Experience shows that by following the ten principles that follow, companies are more likely to arrive at successful business decisions.

Step One: Understand what consensus means.

To reach consensus means to reach a general agreement that all of the decision makers are willing to support.

A consensus agreement does not mean a uniformity of opinion. If decision making required that everyone agree on everything, no decisions would ever be made. No new products would be developed, no buildings built, no partnerships or alliances struck. Consensus decision making is about setting the direction for action—about choosing one alternative rather than others.

Step Two: Keep the decision-making group small.

Consensus decisions are more practical in a group of between four to eight people. A smaller group can readily reach decisions but may lack the insight into the various aspects of the problem that comes from having more than one perspective.

With four to eight people, there is a higher probability of having the experience and skills needed to fully assess alternatives. This number also ensures that enough attention is being paid to the subject. Even if one or two in the group are distracted at the time of the decision, there are likely to be a few who are still focused. With too many people, a consensus on anything becomes impossible. A group of fifteen or more couldn't arrive at a consensus decision about whether or not it was raining.

Step Three: Get a diversity of backgrounds and experiences in the group.

The decision-making group should have members from a sufficient range of experience and backgrounds. The group members should generally be peers, although a group that includes a CEO and next-level VPs can work well. As a general rule, however, it's best to avoid including people who are in supervisor/subordinate relationships to participate in the same decision-making group. Picking group members who have some compatibility of personality or working style is also important. In particular, disruptive personalities can make gaining consensus impossible, even on the easiest decisions.

Step Four: Establish guidelines on the scope of the decision making.

Groups that make effective consensus decisions usually establish guidelines up-front on how decisions will be made. For example, during an effective phase review of a product development effort, a product approval committee will define in advance the questions that need to be answered satisfactorily by a project team in order for them to receive approval to continue into the next phase. The approval committee will go into closed session after the team makes its presentation, and the session will not end until it arrives at a decision to approve the project, cancel it, or redirect the team to do more work on an important issue and come back for approval. This process is so clear that it becomes part of the culture.

TIPS FOR LISTENING EFFECTIVELY FROM A DISTANCE

Read the following for suggestions on how to respond to some problems that might arise when communicating from a distance.

- **Team members are unable to identify with you.** Ask them about a challenge they are currently experiencing and how they plan to solve it; ask them to describe their history and experiences at your company.

- **Team members don't value a relationship with you.** Ask them for their perspective on how effectively the team is functioning; ask for their assistance in helping you better understand what's going on from day to day.

- **Team members seem distracted.** Model for them the behavior you expect during a meeting by closing the door to your office and asking them to do the same; if they work in an open area, ask them to secure an office or conference room so they may communicate with you privately.

- **Team members don't know how to listen.** If you perceive that anyone on your team has difficulty listening, consider this a "red flag" that can probably best be addressed with some group exercises at the next meeting. We suggest this because a group environment tends to be nonthreatening and because it will give anyone you perceive has difficulty listening an opportunity to witness others' techniques and refine their own.

- **Team members are impatient.** Ask them directly what they find to be the sources of their greatest frustration and offer to help them address and solve their frustrations. This might seem simplistic, but don't assume that they've voiced their frustrations already, that anyone has listened if they have, and/or that anyone has at least tried to help them solve their problems.

- **Team members are not ready to listen; it's "not the right time."** If team members are busy or involved in a detailed project with an impending deadline, work with them to schedule a time as soon as possible to communicate privately.

Step Five: Realize that some opinions are more equal than others.

Everyone's opinion should not be equally valued on every issue. Opinions of those who are more experienced or skilled on some issues should carry more weight. For example, the financial vice president may ask questions about the market opportunity for a new product, but would not likely

---

TIPS FOR OFFERING CONSTRUCTIVE FEEDBACK FROM A DISTANCE

When we are contemplating offering constructive feedback, we may have concerns about attendant risks. When communicating from a distance, what techniques might we use to address these possible consequences of giving feedback?

- **Making the situation or relationship worse.** Ask the team member, "What, if any, roadblocks do you see to team success?" Listen as the team member identifies any and all perceived roadblocks, writing each of these down. Next, recite these back and ask the team member to list them in a left-side column of a chart as "Challenges" (as demonstrated in Chapter 7). Next, help this person fill in the right-side column titled "Solutions." Discuss solution options, asking the team member how he or she might ideally solve each challenge. Offer suggestions.

- **Pushing someone over the edge.** Ask an experienced team member or team leader how he or she might approach this particular team member.

- **Generating retaliation, a "counterpunch," or resentment.** Focus discussion with the team member on successes and attendant rewards, including secondary or less emphasis on mistakes and punishments.

- **Being wrong about one's own position or behavior.** Admit to a team member that you have made mistakes; it makes it easier for him or her to do the same.

- **Wasting one's time or energy.** Try a different tack or approach with the team member than you have before; remember, one of the definitions of insanity is taking the same approach to a problem repeatedly and expecting different results.

- **Breaking a cultural norm.** Don't worry about it; mistakes happen; admit a mistake if you make one and move on.

- **Can you say "lawsuit"?** If you believe you are communicating with a team member inclined to file grievances, be careful what you say and document everything.

---

override the opinion of the marketing vice president. The same would be true of how the marketing vice president treats the opinions of the financial vice president on revenue recognition. These team members come together, however, when it's time to weigh the relative importance among different issues.

TIPS FOR MANAGING CONFLICTS FROM A DISTANCE

Sometimes conflicts arise despite all your best efforts. Conflict management from a remote location can require different rules than it does in person. Here are some of the best strategies I've found for remote conflict management.

- **Take resistance seriously; respect its power and energy.** Engage the person who is offering resistance. It might help to involve those from another location in a conference call or videoconference; play the role of questioner and listener, avoiding assertiveness and focusing on your role as a facilitator.

- **Keep the lines of communication open.** In addition to conducting regular meetings, always let those, particularly at other locations, know that you are available for "ad hoc" meetings and/or group calls, with reasonable notice.

- **Don't rush the process.** Be mindful that communication happens in "silos" at each location; when team members engage in communication and/or decision-making processes at one location, require that they share this communication with everyone else on the team. Also, continue to foster, including in remote group discussion, an atmosphere of questioning, reasoning, and discussing as a valuable part of the decision-making process.

- **Be aware of others' or your own resistance.** Listen for verbal signals that resistance is being offered, particularly when communicating with others remotely; encourage others to question you as well if they sense you are offering resistance.

- **Ask what you can learn from the resistance.** This question should be part of your ongoing manager's mantra: "What can I learn from this?"

- **Seek mutual gain (win-win).** Clearly express your desire, particularly in being sensitive to the merger of your team's cultures, that discussions and decision making are not about "who wins" but about "How do we make the best choices, so we all win?"

Step Six: Don't equate compromise with consensus.

The goal is to arrive at the best decision, not one that is acceptable because it satisfies everyone's agenda in some way.

That approach, after all, does not serve the objectives of the business or the needs of the market. And it often leads to mediocrity. There are usually two types of consensus decisions: ones that are relatively easy and ones that are very difficult. Too frequently, the solution to difficult decisions is compromise through give and take.

Step Seven: Prepare sufficiently.

Each member of the decision-making group must be sufficiently prepared. If several members have spent a lot of time trying to understand all aspects of a complex decision and others have not, there is bound to be conflict. Someone with a knowledgeable and carefully considered opinion will not respect an off-the-cuff opinion from someone with little knowledge of the issue. This kind of inequality can cause consensus decision making to break down. When the process breaks down, people find their way around the decisions arrived at in consensus.

Step Eight: Apply consensus decision making to the right types of decisions.

Consensus decision making works best on decisions that are, in effect, approvals, such as when a project team presents a plan for approval of a new product. It does not work well on issues with numerous variations and alternatives that are presented in an unstructured way. Group brainstorming should not be confused with consensus decision making, for example, but it often is. Consensus decision making isn't a quick enough process to reach decisions that have to be made immediately, and it isn't an efficient enough process for small or routine decisions.

Step Nine: Get facilitation if you need it.

Just as any sports team needs coaching before it's ready to play, a management team may need facilitation in consensus decision making. It's interesting how sports teams will practice extensively before they would even think about playing a game, while management teams hardly ever consider practicing before they make real, multimillion-dollar decisions.

One can only speculate on how the course of some companies' fortunes might have changed with a little decision-making practice.

Step Ten: Keep the team playing together.

Just like any sports team, groups that regularly make decisions get remarkably better over time. They build a unique experience base from past decisions and refine the dynamics of how they work together. After a while, a decision-making group can become a real strength within the company, especially if the members don't change regularly.

The dynamics of arriving at a consensus do more than shape better decisions. They enable everyone contributing to the decision to own it: forming a commitment to the decision reached and to its implementation. This is one of the reasons why group consensus decision making increasingly is replacing functional decision making for many management responsibilities. However, like many other management techniques, consensus decision making has to be mastered before you'll be able to use it effectively. Understanding and applying these principles can help your company master this technique and make the decisions that lead to business success and good decisions.

Using Technology

While technology offers many solutions for global teams, it raises questions of its own. What can help team members build trust and understanding and enable them get to know each other better when they cannot easily meet in person? What do we need to understand about cultural differences to choose appropriate technology? How can global team members reduce the frequency and magnitude of misunderstandings that naturally occur on teams? What team communication protocols improve interactions and reduce misunderstandings? How can teams use technology to keep track of what they are doing?

This chapter discusses how to establish trust and understanding on global teams that do not meet in person. We'll look at a range of technologies from teleconferencing, which is the most similar, to meeting face-to-face, to Internet technologies. We provide tips on how to effectively use each of the technologies and how to choose technologies that respect cultural differences. In addition, we suggest how global team leaders can keep informed of the effectiveness of team interactions using Web-based global team assessments.

The groups who have the most difficulty using any technology to conduct meetings will be new teams who have not yet met and teams whose members have a preference for relationship.

The groups who find it easiest are more likely to be the ones who already have met face-to-face and know the others on the team. It helps if they have worked together for some time and have had the opportunity to develop a level of trust and understanding among members of the group. Those who value task higher than they value relationship also adapt to the situation quickly.

Cultural differences play a major role in this phase, since the information people need in order to get a sense of their new colleagues varies significantly from country to country.

While many U.S. team members are primarily interested in the names, positions, and expected roles of their new teammates, people from countries with a higher preference for relationship may also be interested in the ages, marital status, and numbers and ages of the children of their new teammates.

We once worked with a Norwegian licensing negotiation team that was not ready to go to contract with their U.S. colleagues "because we do not know you well enough yet." In order to create an inclusive team atmosphere, team leaders can ask individual team members what information they would like to have about their new teammates, then disseminate that information.

The Technologies

We will now examine several time- and money-saving technologies, focusing on how to use them effectively and with respect for cultural differences.

Videoconferencing

This method of technology creates an experience most akin to personal interaction because it gives team members an opportunity to at least see other team members.

Those included in the conference can watch body language and make some judgments about the congruence between body language and verbal expression. For team members communicating in a second language, visual cues including the ability to see the speaker's mouth make the speaker easier to understand.

What else helps videoconferencing work for global teams? Send out an agenda well before the meeting.

This helps everyone prepare for the meeting, especially those for whom English is not a first language. An agenda sent out a day or so in advance of the meeting will give those who need it an opportunity to look up key words in a dictionary and help them think through what they may wish to offer to the group interaction.

When managing a videoconference, introduce all participants to each other as they join the call. The repetition of participants' names and titles or responsibilities as new members join the call can help team members remember each other.

When discussing any topic, specifically ask for input from each person represented, to ensure that everyone gets a chance to participate and appear on the video screen.

Videoconferencing technology is often administered by someone outside the call. This can relieve the person conducting the meeting, or anyone who is participating, of the anxiety of managing the technology.

Videoconferencing does require that someone in the room manage the camera angles. The picture may jump around a lot due to the number of locations on the call, especially when there are more locations on the call than can be seen at once by the equipment.

Sounds, even coughing or paper shuffling, cause the camera to activate or jump to the location causing the sound. Reduce visual jumping by suggesting that locations put their speakerphones/microphones on mute until it's time to talk.

Teleconferencing

Audio conferencing is much less expensive than videoconferencing. Even small and midsize companies often have this technology in-house. Teleconferencing may make full participation difficult, however, for new team members or those who prefer face-to-face interaction, especially if there are many people they do not know.

Prior to a teleconference, the team leader can suggest that team members call one or two others and introduce themselves in advance. Teams can begin to get acquainted by putting together a series of questions they would like to ask each other and the team leader (including information about their background, whether they know other team members, how long they have been with the company/division/function, where they work, and so on).

Prior to a teleconference, share résumés and photos via the Internet or e-mail, or physically mail a "facebook" or photos of team members. This gives team members a context within which to interact.

Provide presentation materials in advance in electronic or hard-copy format so participants have something to look at while they or others talk.

As with a videoconference, use an agenda and introduce everyone as they join the call. Ask everyone to identify themselves before they speak. Eventually those on the call will get to recognize each voice.

In some cultures, such as in the United States, the usual pattern of speech is to talk over the end of the previous speaker's last sentence. In some cultures, this could be perceived as interrupting. There are cultures (e.g., French) that expect participants to interrupt each other, sometimes even finish the other's thought.

In Asian cultures, specifically, the opposite occurs—there is usually a pause between speakers. People from cultures that value pauses and silence are less likely to interrupt or talk over someone who is finishing. It also means they may never find an opening to say anything unless specifically invited to comment.

As in videoconferencing, audio conference leaders may want to check in with each participant during discussions to encourage each person to participate. Specifically ask those who seem to be just listening if they have additional input. They may be from a culture that values silence or one that comments or responds best only when a leader asks questions. (Also, participants may have been dropped from the call and you may not know unless you ask.) Leaders who expect input from people who may find it difficult to interrupt might assign a topic for comment or report and/or actually put this on the agenda so others respect the time and presentation or report.

Following both video- or audio conferences, send a draft e-mail of meeting minutes that includes agreements and action items. Allow for responses, disagreement, edits, and corrections. Circulate the changes. This helps those for whom the business language is a second language to compare their recollections with formal notes.

Internet Conferencing

The new technology of communicating simultaneously via both telephone and the Internet requires a higher level of sophistication. Internet conferencing enables participants to talk on the telephone while showing Power-Point, Word, or Excel files. Some of the technologies even let any participant on the call take over the presentation and manipulate the application.

To help virtual teams use these interactions effectively, use techniques such as those suggested for teleconferencing. Distribute small photos of each participant on the call. These can sit on the desktop during the conversation so participants can visualize a real person, not just hear a disembodied voice.

Internet conferencing also requires a prepared agenda; PowerPoint slides, Word/Excel files, or other electronic materials; and a technologically savvy support structure. Since users with different versions of operating systems may have difficulty making smooth connections, encourage pre-meeting testing of their connections. Take advantage of the vendors offering pre-meeting support. As with other technologies, follow up via e-mail to confirm agreement by group members and to inform those who could not be at the meeting.

E-mail

When a team is functioning at a high level and has developed trust, e-mail can be an effective means of sharing information. To help teams effectively use e-mail, get them to agree to standards, such as who gets copied on what information; how often information is shared; what goes into the body of the e-mail; what, if anything, gets attached; and finally, what is a reasonable time within which to expect a response.

How one composes the message may be culturally learned (inductive vs. deductive reasoning). Some people prefer to start with the main point of the message and then explain how they arrived at this. Others prefer a chronological report of events that lead up to a conclusion. Some want more details. Others want only an overview.

The focus of the message may vary with the cultural background of the recipient. For example, it is generally considered inappropriate in Germany to include personal information in a professional e-mail. By contrast, e-mail messages to Mexican teammates that only focus on work-related topics might be perceived as cold and aloof and interpreted as lacking interest in the recipient as a person.

Know your audience before you choose a format for the content of your messages. Hold a preliminary conversation among team members to outline a protocol that participants can agree to follow. Global companies, for instance, often include an executive summary in the body of the e-mail (no longer than one page) and attachments providing the details. Some companies post team documents and details from meetings on bulletin boards, in chat rooms, within a knowledge management application, or on a secure intranet site/Web page.

Also, global teams find it useful to agree on who gets included in the "to" line on e-mails, who gets copied, and who is left off the distribution list. People who, because of cultural preferences, are used to a more hierarchical relationship with superiors (this cultural dimension is called "power distance") are more likely to include the boss on a "cc" (e.g., in France). Other team members from more-participative cultures might view copying the superior as an effort to tattle to the boss or cover one's own tracks.

Internet Technologies

Savvy global team leaders may set up team Web pages. On these pages include some personal information such as pictures of team members (and perhaps their families) and a brief description of the team members' outside interests. You may also include descriptions of each team member's past and present work, and characteristics of successful teams on which each team member has worked in the past. This approach is particularly well suited to teams that include people from Latin America, Latin Europe, Eastern Europe, and the Far East. Specific information about educational background is generally valued more highly in Asia and Europe than in the United States, unless the person graduated from an Ivy League school or received an MBA.

Scheduled Web-based teamwork postings can provide global team leaders with updates available to them at a time convenient to their work-day. Web-based team measurement tools also can be used to collect data on team interactions. Such data can help the team leader identify team interactions that need his or her attention.

Electronic Meeting Options

For the really tech-savvy teams, there are electronic meeting options:

- Instant messaging services allow people to exchange e-mails simultaneously. (The application automatically notifies a specific list of people whenever one is on the Internet or e-mail.)
- Chat rooms allow moderated or unmoderated real-time discussions to take place online. (This should be limited to team members only.)
- Bulletin boards are more typically used for posting a question or topic to which others post electronic comments or responses.

For certain teams working on the same project in different countries or different time zones, use of electronic meeting applications can spur information sharing and instigate valuable discussions that might not have happened without the technology.

Additional Considerations

Respecting Differences

Be very careful when asking about the technology levels and experience of your foreign colleagues. Some U.S. team members have seriously offended people overseas with questions like, "Don't you guys have e-mail?"

Also, as in the United States, the use of technology may come more easily to the younger generation, while the older generation still may be the team leaders or decision makers.

Watching Your Time

Sensitivity to time zone differences also supports good global team process. A late morning meeting in the United States can occur in the middle of the night for someone in Asia and late afternoon or early evening for someone in Eastern or even Western Europe. Global meetings using technology almost always have someone participating at an hour that is not convenient or within his or her regular work hours.

Sensitivity to meeting times goes a long way to helping team members from locations other than company headquarters feel respected. Too often, even for face-to-face meetings, it is always the same people who have to come to team meetings, real or virtual, outside their regular work schedule.

This can send the message that these team members are less important (and therefore can be inconvenienced more often than others on the team). Varying the meeting times and sometimes scheduling meetings at times inconvenient for the leader means a great deal to team members elsewhere.

Measuring Team Interactions

Whether or not technology is the primary means of communication among team members, establishing communication protocols, especially by including all team members in the discussion to share their preferences, will go a long way to reducing the frequency and magnitude of misunderstandings that regularly crop up in global or virtual settings.

Team issues can range from not understanding communication protocols (for example, who gets copied on written documents), to decision making, leadership, and conflict resolution. The level of complexity increases on global teams where one's expectations for how each of these should be handled may also be culturally biased.

What is expected of a team leader varies significantly from culture to culture. For example, you may find that a team leader of Russians may be expected to give specific instructions as to what team members are supposed to do, when, and how. Many U.S. team members would consider these instructions as "marching orders" or micromanagement. By contrast, the leader of a Swedish team may seem, by American standards, more like a coach. In the cases described here, a team leader who wants to be effective might need to adopt a more directive style when working with his or her Russian team members, and probably should "back off" when working with the Swedish team.

However, only those team leaders who regularly measure the human process interactions among team members can effectively manage, without travel, team issues over great distances. Issues likely to arise on co-located teams are often magnified for teams dispersed across the globe.

Knowing when there are issues, analyzing the causes, and identifying solutions early—when problems remain small—can mean the difference between the failure and success of a virtual or global team. The new global order may require data collection from team members worldwide, using electronic questionnaires and assessment products. Gathering input from the team, providing results, and discussing what the team members think about how to make necessary changes will facilitate improvement in team effectiveness and productivity.

Since global teams represent a significant corporate investment, periodically measuring teams who cannot meet together is a proactive way to protect this investment. Team leaders unable to visit all locations find increasing value in periodic measurement and structured discussion around team issues and improvements. More and more turn to collection of data and dissemination of results over the Internet prior to team discussions.

Conclusion

As companies pull back on travel, global teams replace face-to-face meetings with remote interactions via telecommunications or the Internet. Team leaders need to ensure that their teams use the right electronic tools to facilitate project work. Team leaders need to pay close attention to the needs of team members, particularly when the team includes people from very different cultural backgrounds. They need to adapt their leadership style to the needs of their teammates; and team members need to be mindful of the style preferences of their team leaders and react accordingly. Team leaders need to test their own assumptions for cultural biases when considering whether communication within the team is effective, how to delegate work, and how to resolve issues.

Since cultural differences are often hard to identify, quarterly measurement of the human process interactions provides the team leader with important data. This approach also facilitates regular communication among team members on team process. It sets the stage for the leader to step in early to identify and help the team resolve issues before these issues negatively impact the team's output.

Global team leaders who effectively use technology to "meet" with their team, measure team interactions, look for and address cultural differences, and talk through work issues, can dramatically improve team effectiveness and efficiency with minimal international travel.

Last but not least, a coaching refresher. . . .

CHAPTER TWELVE

Motivating the Masses: How to Be a Great Coach

Y OUR FINAL RESPONSIBILITY AS A manager is to help your employees keep up when they may be struggling—for any reason, from diminished resources to increased responsibility to conflict with colleagues. Sometimes it's a personal matter that's interfering with their concentration on the job. Whatever the problem is, the following is an RSI- and HPE-based framework for uncovering the cause, setting the necessary goals to overcome it, and helping your employee get back on track. Effective coaching is the difference between good managers and great ones, so don't underestimate its importance to your team's success.

Initial statement of the coaching need

Initial statement of goals (including measures)

The person being coached (the "Client") wants . . .

I want . . .

Relationship logistics

Relating I—Assessment of Coaching Subject's Physical, Emotional, and Intellectual Needs

Physical

Posture

Facial expressions

Grooming

Behaviors

Emotional

This person's use of words to express feelings or emotions?

This person's reaction to my use of feeling words?

Intellectual

Grasp of content?

Systematic problem-solving approach?

Inferences

How would I describe this person's mental state?

How would I describe this person's interaction style?

Relating II—Assessment of Person, Content, and Context

Person

Knowledge

Skills

Abilities

Personal Characteristics

Content

Does the appropriate level of content (data, concepts, principles, applications, objectives) exist?

Is the content accurate?

Context

Are there rewards for the desired behavior?

Are there punishments for the desired behavior?

Are there rewards for wrong behavior?

Are there punishments for wrong behavior?

Relating III—Responding

Where am I emotionally regarding this relationship?

Where am I intellectually regarding this person's issues?

What is my style and how must I flex to work with this person?

What are the next steps?

For them?

For me?

TIPS FOR EFFECTIVE COACHING FROM A DISTANCE

To get everyone "on the same page," try these tips:

- Once a week, communicate the same written message (via e-mail) to everyone on your team. This way, everyone is literally getting the same message from you on a regular, weekly basis.

- Once a week, every two weeks, and/or once a month, meet with at least your managers and supervisors. Communicate your team goals verbally and in writing.

To get everyone to a "meeting" of some sort, try these tips:

- Give everyone permission to participate.

- If your department's work includes "customer-critical" and/or "vital" functions (e.g., keeping the power running, operations, and/or functions considered "life sustaining"), either hold two meetings relatively proximate to one another which cover the same content or hold one meeting for which managers and supervisors are held accountable for discussing the meeting's content ASAP in a team meeting.

- Try to conduct a meeting very early in the day, before the real "heat" of the workday occurs.

To ensure that, when people in one location engage in a work-related problem-solving conversation, they share the content of what they discussed with those at other locations, try these tips:

- Set expectations and establish a process where, perhaps at each team meeting involving managers and supervisors, managers and supervisors at each location are responsible for reporting to the team at large these discussions.

- Set expectations and establish a process where, after these sorts of discussions occur, one person in that group is responsible for reporting the content to everyone on the team.

- Establish, using your team's department intranet, a "place" where team members can post "Best Practices," "Problem-Solving Tips," and/or "FAQs" (Frequently Asked Questions).

To help manage team members who are at a distance as effectively as those you manage face-to-face, try these tips:

- Establish a set "face-to-face" schedule for group or individual meetings with those you manage at locations other than your "home" location.

- Establish a set schedule for one-on-one phone conversations with your team members in other locations.

- Establish a set schedule for group conversations with your team members at other locations.

Remember, this book is designed to help you address ten team performance aspects:

1. Managing a team
2. Customer service
3. Communication
4. Facilitating change
5. Removing troublemakers
6. Managing your boss
7. Clashes between two teams
8. Managing performance
9. Budgeting
10. Taking a team from any of three stages to peak performance

Don't try to tackle all ten of these topics today. Choose the three that are most important to you and start working on them; the other seven will "fall in line" as you see fit and prioritize. The keys to managerial success include:

1. Don't allow yourself to be overwhelmed—Prioritize Your Top Three.
2. Work your Top Three Priorities first—Prioritizing (still).
3. Schedule how and when you will address the other seven priorities (first day, first week, first month, first quarter)—90-Day Planning.
4. Work everything in the order that suits you—Effective Execution.

When you prioritize, plan, and execute in this fashion, you significantly increase the likelihood that you will be managing and facilitating significant improvement in team performance within the next 90 days . . .

90 Days to a High-Performance Team!

Index